MW00743700

ONLY RIBS

BABY BACK RIB RECIPES

A COOKBOOK
by QUENTIN ERICKSON

ONLY RIBS: BABY BACK RIB RECIPES

Published by Entrée Press, LLC.

Copyright © 2011 Entrée Press, LLC. All rights reserved.

No part of the contents of this publication may be reproduced or transmitted by any means, electronic, mechanical, photocopying, recording, or otherwise without the written permission of Entrée Press, LLC.

ONLY RIBS: BABY BACK RIB RECIPES

ISBN 978-0-9773344-4-5

Printed in the United States of America

No liability is assumed with respect to the use of the information contained herein. Although all reasonable efforts have been made to present accurate information in the preparation of this publication, no guarantees, including expressed or implied warranties, are made with respect to this information by the publisher and author who also assume no legal responsibility for the accuracy of presentations, comments or other information, including any errors or omissions in this publication. The user is encouraged to seek out additional information on the proper handling of food and cooking safety from other sources if any questions or concerns arise. In addition, no liability is assumed and all liability is expressly declined for damages resulting from the use, misuse, or failure to use the information contained herein. Please use common sense, and always err on the side of safety.

Products and company names mentioned herein may be the trademarks of their respective owners.

For my wonderful wife, Mary, and my sons, Rene and Alex,
who have joined me over the course of many years,
enthusiastically, on this culinary journey.

And a sincere thank you to Doug Schenkelberg,
my all-weather friend, who, for this project, provided consultation
and sound advice on various aspects of cooking and recipes.

QUENTIN ERICKSON, is a globe-trotting, life-long foodie and improvisational cook who is bringing his mantra *"Variety in food is the spice of life!"* to all who love culinary adventure. His exploratory cookbooks focus on the myriad of options and wealth of inspiration available to us all.

Entrée Press Online

Visit www.EntreePress.com to explore additional "Play with your food!" interactive cookbooks.

CONTENTS

THE FIRST BITE

GRILLED BABY BACK RIBS

OVEN COOKED BABY BACK RIBS

STOVE TOP BABY BACK RIBS

SLOW COOKER BABY BACK RIBS

APPENDIX   133

NOTES

THE FIRST BITE

"Cooking is like love. It should be entered into with abandon or not at all."
Harriet Van Horne

"I feel a recipe is only a theme, which an intelligent cook can play each time with a variation."
Madame Benoit

These two quotes eloquently encapsulate my personal philosophy on cooking and the intent of this cookbook. Cooking, like life, is a great adventure that should be undertaken with great gusto.

My hobby over the years has been collecting and cooking recipes, with a focus on the unusual, the outlandish and the novel. Early on, I found that I derived more satisfaction from experimentation than with following the "paint-by-numbers" method.

Substituting ingredients, altering ingredient amounts, changing cooking methods—it has all become a happy obsession. Some basic kitchen and grilling equipment, a well-stocked pantry and a vivid imagination can result in stellar cuisine.

As a result of this on-going experimentation, I have become a better cook, I have a lot more fun in the kitchen, and my palate has become much more refined. I believe that you too can achieve these same benefits by embracing an adventurous attitude. These recipes should be seen as the jumping-off point of *your* great adventure.

Explore, experiment, be bold and find inspiration in the subtle and the obvious. Cooking, as is life, is a journey whose path can be both sweet and savory and whose destination is satisfaction. When you pour your heart and soul into cooking, the rewards are immense.

Quentin

USING THE COOKBOOK

As I experiment with my recipes, I do a pretty fair job of documenting substitutions and other alterations I've made, although sometimes the scribbles can be a bit indecipherable. The page formatting of the recipes in this collection is intended to directly assist you on your journey of exploration. Use these pages to shop for ingredients, capture the thoughts of dinner guests, document cooking dates, and most importantly, record your experimentation for future reference.

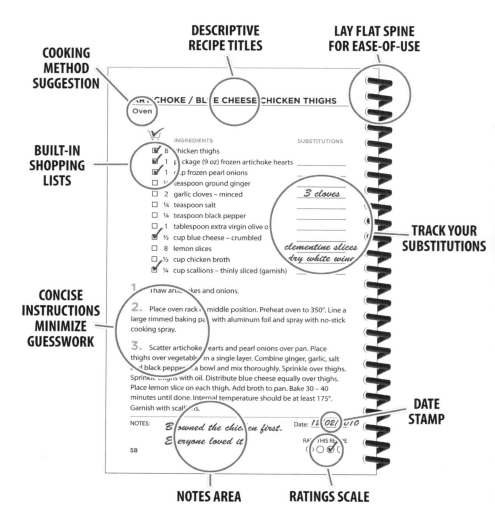

DESCRIPTIVE RECIPE TITLES

LAY FLAT SPINE FOR EASE-OF-USE

COOKING METHOD SUGGESTION

BUILT-IN SHOPPING LISTS

CONCISE INSTRUCTIONS MINIMIZE GUESSWORK

TRACK YOUR SUBSTITUTIONS

DATE STAMP

NOTES AREA

RATINGS SCALE

PLAY WITH YOUR FOOD

The ingredient, flavoring and cooking process combinations available to you are virtually infinite, bounded only by the ingredients you happen to have on hand. Take advantage of that variety. Recipes are but a framework to build upon and to deviate from, to alter and to modify to your own tastes and satisfaction.

Make adjustments and refinements to the recipe until the dish is perfect for you. It is a dash to the cupboard for spices, to the refrigerator for new ingredients or to the wine rack for a splash of wine. Experiment, enjoy, fail and then prevail. Innovate, experiment, compare recipes, combine recipes, feed the failures to the dog and the successes to royalty (your in-laws). Be bold. Do. Try. Win!

SUBSTITUTION REVOLUTION

Your primary method for creating culinary creations unique to you and your tastes is through ingredient substitution. Substitutions can have a subtle or profound impact on the flavor profile, texture, healthiness and even the cooking time of recipes. By fully embracing experimentation and improvisation, you will have more fun in the kitchen while becoming a better cook, you'll develop a more sophisticated palate, and you'll create a collection of recipes that are uniquely yours.

There are other reasons you might want to substitute an ingredient (other than for the sheer enjoyment of tasting your successful creations). You may have health concerns, you may be missing an ingredient, or you may not like a particular taste.

In the appendix, you'll find a wealth of information that will get you going in the right direction. The material is not exhaustive, nor is it meant to be. It represents only a small portion of the options available to you, but it will be a solid reference for you in your adventures. Use your imagination, improvise, explore!

PLAYING DRESS-UP

Diners eat first with their eyes. If your food looks unappetizing, you've gotten off on the wrong taste bud. The way your meal is presented affects the way the diners think the food will taste.

The Plan

Preplan the presentation of the dish from the time you begin its preparation. Have a visualization of the completed meal in mind. If you are serving hot food, plating has to be done quickly. Consider building a "practice plate" before plating all the meals.

The Plate

Use a plate large enough to allow you to use "white space" as a design element. You don't want to crowd the food. Allow the food to "breathe" on the plate. Plates that are white or neural in color will allow the food to stand front and center. The shape of the plate should be simple as well. The focus should always be on the food.

Consider heating the plates in an electric oven if that particular food combination can benefit from a warm plate that keeps the components warm during serving and on into the meal. Preheat the oven to 150° and warm the plates for 5 minutes or so. Be extra careful handling the hot plates.

Pay attention to how the plate will be oriented when served. Use the front of the plate to highlight the main focus of the meal. If you are going to add height to the food, placing the height at the back of the plate will add to the appeal.

Plating

First and foremost, keep it simple. Unless you have a kitchen staff, you are going to want to be able to plate quickly, while the food is still hot. Start from the middle of the plate and work your way outward. Don't fuss too much with the plated food, you'll only make things worse.

COLOR: Select foods that add visual interest through color. Poultry and fish can have fairly bland colors. Colorful vegetables, peppers and fruit wedges can add that splash of color the plate is calling for.

SHAPE: Take the shape of the foods into consideration. Round meatballs, round Brussels sprouts and round potatoes on a plate do not an exciting plate make. Take a few moments to cut and shape the food into different figures and sizes to create visual appeal.

SYMMETRY: The house says odd always beats even: five meatballs are more pleasing to the eye than four; three colors on a plate are more interesting than two. Apply this maxim to any plating variable.

TEXTURE: Though not a visual presentation element, don't neglect texture. A well balanced plate requires variety in texture. Puréed squash, baked salmon and whipped potatoes may taste great together but will not provide any variety in mouth feel.

SAUCES: Go easy on the sauce, as too much sauce on the plate may give the impression that you are trying to hide a poorly prepared meal. Sauces are generally placed underneath the meat. If you lean the meat against the starch element of the meal, you'll keep the meat from becoming too saturated in the sauce, and the diner will better be able to view its preparation.

NEATNESS: And finally, take the time to be sure your plates are neat and free of drips and spills. No slopped sauces or stray pieces—your finished plate should be a work of art, with you the acclaimed artist.

Garnishes

Garnishes provide a great opportunity for adding that dash of panache. A quick shave of parmesan cheese, a sprig of parsley or cilantro, a wedge of avocado, a dollop of sour cream, a dash of paprika—all just a taste of the available garnishes. Garnishes are just the right touch of color, texture and flavor. All garnishes should be of the edible variety—avoid items like rosemary sprigs or flower pedals, for instance.

Inspiration

As always, inspiration is where you find it. Look to food magazines for ideas on arranging food on the plate, pay attention to the plating techniques at your favorite restaurant, and experiment with your own plates. You are only limited by attentiveness and imagination.

TO GRILL OR NOT TO GRILL

Rib tartare is not an option. We know that pork has to be cooked somehow. This cookbook provides suggested cooking methods for each recipe. These are only suggestions! Altering cooking methods is another opportunity for experimentation. These rib recipes are generally interchangeable between oven, grill and slow cooker.

When cooking pork ribs in the oven, a relatively steady, even, medium temperature produces the best result. Ribs should not be cooked too quickly as they can become tough and dry.

If you plan on translating grill or oven recipes to the slow cooker, here are suggested recipe modifications:

- Reduce liquids by about 25 percent. There is very little evaporation in slow cooking.

- Reduce by approximately one half the recommended quantity of whole leaves and spices. Add additional herbs and spices in the last hour of cooking for a flavor boost.

Whichever cooking method you choose, the internal temperature of pork baby back ribs should be at least 160°. Use a meat thermometer to ensure doneness.

TIME OUT

Different situations can influence cooking times. For example, not all ovens are accurate—they can vary by many degrees plus or minus the set temperature. You will need to learn the idiosyncrasies of your particular oven.

Foods cook more slowly at higher altitudes, so depending on the nature of your oven and your altitude, cooking times could vary by as much as 20%.

If you use a convection oven, cooking times will definitely be different from those of a conventional oven. Refer to the manufacturers' recommendations about cooking times.

Cooking times for bone-in meats is longer as the bone absorbs a lot of heat and does not conduct heat effectively.

Meat that has been brined will cook more quickly. There is speculation that the extra moisture in the tissue, with its high heat conductivity qualities, accelerates the cooking process.

Other factors that influence cooking time include the thickness of the cut, temperature of the meat when you begin cooking, how many times you open the cooking equipment to take a peek, the quantity of other foods being cooked at the same time, and the fat content of the item being cooked.

A meat thermometer is now standard equipment for every kitchen. If you don't have one, pick one up the next time you leave the house! Using a meat thermometer is quite straight forward: place the probe in the thickest part of the cut and away from bone. See Table 5 in the Appendix for recommended safe internal temperatures for cooked meats.

FINDING YOUR STYLE

Perhaps the most enjoyable aspect of constant exploration and improvisation, other than the well-deserved accolades of dinner guests, is that through exploration you will be developing your own voice, your own brand of confidence, your own style.

"Style" in cooking has many faces. Do you prefer the comfort provided by comfort food and a satisfied brood? Do you concentrate on healthy fare and fresh produce? Does your idea of cooking involve stoking coals and managing the temperature of a grill, regardless of mother nature's plans?

Do you prefer quick and easy meals, your pantry overflowing with instant potatoes, instant rice and instant gratification? Do you prefer cooking everything from scratch, time at the market and in the kitchen be damned? Are you a study in culinary improvisation, working without a net, your pantry stocked with imported spices and exotic concoctions?

Do you define your style by an American regional cuisine? Cajun? New England? Southwestern? Or perhaps you prefer cooking with an international flair. French? Italian? Mexican? Szechuan?

Your individual cooking style will have elements of all of these definitions, and will continue to refine itself over time. As you develop your "style," be sure to place an emphasis on expanding your horizons. By bringing in influences from many sources, you'll develop a sense of the compatibility of different tastes, you will learn to intuitively develop your own recipes, and in the process, you will find more joy in the kitchen.

THE FLAVOR FRONTIER

YOU HAVE GOOD TASTE

You have good taste. That much is obvious—you're reading this cookbook! Developing your culinary palate will (and should) be a life-long endeavor, and you should consider it one of the most gratifying journeys you will embark upon in life. I consider the ongoing development of my palate to be one of my life's great journeys.

Developing your palate is not as difficult as you might think. And it is not necessarily just about trying new foods. You can start by trying different varieties of foods you already enjoy. There are literally hundreds of varieties of cheeses, and multiple varieties of many basic vegetables. Go with what you know.

But eventually you will need to venture into the unknown. Give new and novel (to you) food the benefit of the doubt, and admit that someone, somewhere, must believe a particular item to be at least edible or it probably wouldn't be considered "food."

You may find delicious treats that you never knew existed, and you may find some food items that for you will be an acquired taste. Acquire that taste. A great pleasure of mine is turning palate-shy people into Brussels sprout eaters. Boiled until tender (the sprouts, not the people), sliced open and stuffed with blue cheese, crumbled bacon, and a grain or two of sea salt, then drizzled with olive oil and broiled until the cheese is bubbling—avowed sprouts haters will be lining up for the recipe!

Stop smoking, brush your tongue.

And finally, the more information you have, the better equipped you are to explore the culinary landscape. Seminars, foodie magazines, television shows, restaurants—inspiration is where you find it. Explore. Climb. Conquer!

1-2-3 TRINITY

A "trinity" is the combination of three essential ingredients as the flavoring base in a recipe, often created by sautéing a combination of any three aromatic vegetables, condiments, seasonings, herbs, or spices. Trinities are most typically used when creating sauces, soups, stew, and stir-fries.

Geographic regions often have a trinity of ingredients that comprise the flavor base of dishes for that cuisine. For example, if the recipe calls for a base of onion, bell pepper and celery it is a good bet it is a Louisiana Creole dish. This particular trinity combination is known as the "Holy Trinity." Create your own regional dishes by experimenting with "trinity" combinations of ingredients. See Table 6 in the Appendix for a list of trinity flavor bases from various cultures.

COOKING WITH HEAT

To regulate the heat in a recipe, increase or decrease any of the heat ingredients listed here. With the exception of horseradish and wasabi, they are chili pepper-based.

- Hot pepper sauce is a primary heat source in many recipes. It is basically chili peppers combined with tomatoes, onions, vinegar, sugar and spices.

- Cayenne pepper is a powder derived from several different chilies to produce a hot, fiery taste.

- Red pepper flakes are available as whole flakes, ground red pepper flakes or crushed red pepper flakes.

- Harissa sauce is a product from north Africa. It is flavorful and hot. It is made up of hot chili peppers, cumin, coriander, garlic, caraway and oil.

- Sriracha is the name of a hot sauce with a southeast Asian influence. It is a hot chili sauce made from dried chilies ground into a paste with garlic, vinegar, salt, sugar and other ingredients.

- Horseradish, commercially prepared, is recommended in this cookbook because it is handy and convenient. For a real jolt, though, try freshly-grated horseradish root.

- Wasabi, horseradish's Japanese cousin, will give a good jolt, too.

The heat of peppers can be softened by removing the seeds and ribs from the inside, but the flesh will still be hot. In general, the smaller the pepper and the narrower the shoulder near the stem, the hotter the bite, but some varieties will break the rules with a fiery surprise.

When working with fiery peppers, it's important to protect yourself by using eye protection and wearing latex or rubber gloves. After handling peppers, wash your hands carefully with plenty of soap and warm water before touching your eyes and mouth.

In the event the heat surpasses your tolerance level, a cold glass of milk—not water—can have a mitigating effect on the condition. Milk contains the protein casein which pulls the capsaicin (the active heat component of chili peppers) away from the burning taste buds. See Table 7 in the Appendix for a list of capsaicin levels in different peppers.

RUBS AND MARINADES AND BRINES, OH MY!

Rubs

Spice rubs can add a great deal of flavor to meat or fish dishes. The spices are generally course ground, and the mixture can also include various herbs, salt and crushed garlic. Adding sugar will cause the rub to caramelize during cooking. Adding oil will create a paste, which can help the rub adhere to the meat. Rubs are readily available at the supermarket, but creating your own is much more rewarding. Rubs can be sweet, spicy and everything in between. If you are adventurous, rubs on vegetables can be delicious.

Generally, the rub should not be applied any sooner than two hours before cooking, although some recipes recommend longer times. The rationale for applying the rub just before cooking is to eliminate the chance of the rub inducing texture changes in the meat.

I've found that brushing the food item with spicy mustard just prior to applying the rub not only helps the rub stick but also adds complexity of flavor.

Place the food item on a cooking rack and lay newspaper under the rack. The rub should be applied generously. What sticks on, sticks on, and what falls off, falls off. I have found that using a pizza red pepper flake shaker works great for dispensing the rub. Gently massaging the rub onto the surface will increase the amount of rub that adheres. Apply the rub to the top, bottom and edges of the food item. Minimize handling—the more you fuss, the more the rub will fall off. Reapply the spices that dropped onto the newspaper to minimize waste.

Marinades

Marinating is the process of flavoring food by soaking in heavily seasoned liquid before cooking. A marinade can be acidic if based on liquids such as vinegar or lemon juice, or enzymatic if made with ingredients such as papaya or pineapple.

The maximum marinating time for poultry, under any circumstances, is 3 hours. Any longer than 3 hours and the meat will become mushy. I recommend 8 hours marinating for ribs. Marinade can be used to tenderize tough cuts of meats, but marinate times are quite long when trying to tenderize (up to 24 hours), so is recommended for only the toughest cuts.

Flavors can be enhanced with sweeteners such as sugar, honey and syrups. Soy sauce is a fantastic marinade ingredient. Herbs and spices commonly used in marinating are oil-soluble and their flavor is released when mixed with oil.

When marinating, use a jumbo re-sealable plastic bag to hold the marinade and meat. Before placing the bag in the refrigerator, set the bag on a plate to avoid a mess in the event of a bag leak. If the ribs are too large for the bag, cut the ribs to fit. If jumbo bags are not available, any container will work if it can be sealed tightly.

Brines

Like marinating, brining is a process in which poultry, pork or seafood is soaked in a liquid solution before cooking. Meats with high fat content like beef, lamb and duck, tend not to benefit from brining. The basic brine is salt, sugar and water. I prefer sea salt and brown sugar, as they impart more flavor. Combine the ingredients in a ratio of 1 cup salt, 1 cup sugar to 2 quarts water.

Determine how much brine you'll need to completely submerge the food item in your selected, sealable container. Mix the salt, sugar and water (plus any other spices) together, heat the mixture to dissolve the salt and sugar, and let cool completely. Combine the brine and food in the container, and then place a ceramic plate or bowl on the food to submerge it, and place in the fridge. For large items like a whole turkey, use a cooler, adding ice to the cooler to keep it chilled for 8 to 12 hours. For small birds or poultry portions, brine for around 3 hours, and for pork chops or tenderloins, brine for around 6 hours.

The salt in the brine works to hydrate the cells of the muscle tissue by drawing water into the tissues through osmosis, and also denatures the cell proteins, further helping the meat to retain moisture during cooking.

Regardless of the science involved, it works! If you've never brined a turkey, you've missed a moist, mystical experience. Because a brine opens up the meat to hydration, if you add other herbs and spices to the brine, these additional flavor additives with also deeply infuse into the meat.

INSPIRATION IS WHERE YOU FIND IT

I traveled the globe during my hitch in the Navy, and I traveled the width and breadth of the United States in my decades-long civilian career. I have been privileged to experience a bounty of diverse foods and cultures, and to share those experiences with many friends, customers and employees.

Some "not-to-be-forgotten" culinary experiences include:

- A black bean soup in Indianapolis, Indiana
- Crawfish in restaurants along Lake Pontchartrain, Louisiana
- Baby back ribs in San Antonio, Texas
- A turtle soup in St. Louis, Missouri
- A steak flambé in a second-story restaurant overlooking the Ramblas in Barcelona, Spain
- Oysters in a bar in Athens, Greece
- Abalone on the wharf in San Francisco, California
- A crème brûlée at the Ritz-Carlton in Chicago, Illinois
- A gumbo in Greenfield, North Carolina
- A hearts of palm salad at the Breakers Hotel in West Palm Beach, Florida
- A rack of lamb in Neenah, Wisconsin
  - . . . and the list goes on

I ate fine and not-so-fine food as I dined at a myriad of restaurants and resorts. These experiences all had an impact on my personal cooking style. Always, I would try to choose a menu item that would give me a new experience. These unique dishes provided ideas and inspiration. Inspiration is where you find it. Use the skills of others to your own advantage.

WRESTLING RECIPES

LOOK BEFORE YOU LEAP

A highly recommended practice is to scan and survey a recipe before cooking it. You don't want to find midway though cooking that you are missing a key ingredient or that you are about to add an ingredient you don't like! Gather your ingredients and plan your substitutions.

A PLACE FOR EVERYTHING

The French term "mise en place" literally means "putting in place." For us it means organizing and arranging all ingredients for a recipe, prior to cooking, and placing them in the food preparation area in the order listed in the recipe. I also pre-measure all the ingredients and place them in small bowls or cups to use in sequence as I prepare a recipe.

ANYONE CAN ADD, BUT CAN YOU SUBTRACT?

It is simple to revise the profile of a recipe by adding or adjusting ingredients. Once all the ingredients are mixed, however, it is very difficult to eliminate or mask a flavor. Exercise a bit of caution when substituting ingredients — add a bit at a time and taste as you go.

POKE ME IN THE RIBS

BABY BACK RIBS

Eating ribs is always an enjoyable experience. You get to eat with your hands, lick your fingers, and if your face is covered in sauce, no one seems to mind. Eating ribs that you've cooked yourself, with loving care and careful attention to flavors, is a whole different level of fun.

There are different types of rib cuts available—spare ribs, St. Louis style, country style and many more. The cuts get their names from where on the pig rib cage the cut is taken. Baby back ribs are taken from the top of the rib cage. They are shorter, curved, and have tender, tasty meat between and on top of the bones. The designation "baby" indicates the cuts are from market weight hogs.

A typical commercial rack is 10-13 ribs. A rack will feed one to two people. As you shop for rib racks, look for lean, large racks with a lot of meat (1¾ pounds or more). Look for racks that are brightly colored. Previously frozen ribs should be your last choice. Fresh ribs have a distinctly better flavor.

I've found that a good method for cooking baby back ribs is in the oven at 325° for 40 – 50 minutes. A second method is to slow cook ribs in the oven or with indirect heat on the grill. Temperature should be maintained at around 275° for 3 – 4 hours. My third preferred method is direct grilling.

Whichever method is chosen, monitor cooking of baby back ribs closely. Baby back ribs cook quicker than do other styles. Use a meat thermometer to ensure they are cooked through to a safe internal temperature.

NICE RIB RACK

Most home grills are not large enough to hold multiple racks of ribs flat on the cooking grate. A grilling rib rack can hold up to four racks of ribs in an upright position and is a recommended piece of grilling equipment.

INSANE MEMBRANE

The back side of ribs has a connective tissue membrane sometimes referred to as "silverskin." It is tough, tasteless and inedible and should be removed before marinating and cooking:

- Insert a knife as far as possible under the membrane on the wider end of rack.
- Use paper toweling or pliers to help grip the membrane.
- Loosen it and pull it back an inch or two. Grab the membrane and then tug firmly to pull it slowly away from the entire rack.

PROPER PREP

- All recipes in this collection are designed to serve 4 people.
- Wash hands before and after handling ribs
- Trim excess fat. Rinse ribs to remove extraneous material and pat dry with paper towels. Thoroughly dry the rib racks to achieve proper browning. Rinsing does not kill bacteria— cooking to 160° kills bacteria.

- Rib racks may be cut into halves, quarters or individual ribs for convenient handling. Sometimes rib racks must be sized to fit the available cooking equipment. Keep rib racks as whole as possible, subdividing only when necessary.

- Use a jumbo re-sealable plastic bag or a 1-gallon re-sealable plastic bag when marinating ribs. Squeeze out excess air before sealing bag.

COOKING TIPS FOR RIBS

- Marinating time for ribs is 8 or more hours

- When grilling with low-indirect heat, promote a moist and juicy rack of ribs by adding water to an aluminum pan set directly on the coal grate. When oven roasting, promote a moist and juicy rack of ribs by placing a shallow pan of water on the bottom oven rack.

- Searing ribs is best accomplished when the grill is at its hottest. Place meat over the high temperature area. Sear ribs two minutes. Turn and sear the other side for two minutes. Turn ribs (and baste, if part of recipe) frequently.

- Monitor cooking of ribs until the meat is no longer pink, juices run clear and internal temperature is at least 160°. Use a meat thermometer to obtain precise temperatures. The cooking times recommended in these recipes are approximations.

- Different sizes and shapes of ribs will require different cooking times. For best results, uniform rib racks should be cooked together as different sizes require different cooking times.

- When using the slow cooker, refrain from lifting the lid. Condensation is part of the cooking process.

- When ribs are fully cooked, remove from heat and rest by placing them on a clean platter and tenting with aluminum foil. Letting the ribs rest 5 – 10 minutes will allow juices to meld with the meat.

SAFETY FIRST

- Internal temperature of pork baby back ribs should be at least 160° with no observable pink. Monitor cooking carefully. Use a meat thermometer for an accurate measurement. The cooking times recommended in recipes are approximations.

- Once cooked, ribs should be kept either hot or promptly refrigerated or frozen. Cooked ribs can be refrigerated for up to two days.

- Frozen uncooked ribs should be used within two or three months of freezing. Frozen cooked ribs should be used within one month.

- Reheat ribs in a covered baking dish in a 375° oven or in a microwave set on high until meat internal temperature is 165°.

NOTES

GRILLED
BABY BACK RIBS

APPLESAUCE BABY BACK RIBS

Marinate | Grill 1 Hour

		INGREDIENTS	SUBSTITUTIONS
☐	3 – 4	pounds baby back ribs (2 meaty racks)	
☐	½	teaspoon salt	_____
☐	1	teaspoon black pepper	_____
☐	1	teaspoon cumin	_____
☐	1	teaspoon cayenne pepper	_____
☐	2	garlic cloves – minced	_____
☐	3	cups barbecue sauce	_____
☐	3	cups applesauce	_____
☐	½	tablespoon liquid smoke	_____

1. Combine salt, black pepper, cumin, cayenne pepper and garlic in a bowl and mix thoroughly. Massage ribs evenly with rub. Cut rib racks in half.

2. Combine barbecue sauce, applesauce and liquid smoke in bowl. Place rib racks in jumbo re-sealable plastic bag. Pour sauce into bag, seal and toss to coat ribs thoroughly. Marinate in refrigerator 8 or more hours.

3. Spray grill grate with no-stick cooking spray. Prepare grill for low-direct heat. Place ribs in a double wrap of aluminum foil and seal. Place foil pack on grill and cook ribs 45 minutes. Remove ribs from foil and grill uncovered 15 – 35 minutes until done. Maintain grill temperature at 300°. Internal temperature of ribs should be at least 160°.

NOTES: Date: _____

RATE THIS RECIPE
○ ○ ○ ○ ○

BARBECUE SAUCE BABY BACK RIBS

Grill 3 – 4 Hours

		INGREDIENTS	SUBSTITUTIONS
☐	3 – 4	pounds baby back ribs (2 meaty racks)	
☐	1½	cups barbecue sauce	_____
☐	2	tablespoons molasses	_____
☐	2	tablespoons brown sugar	_____
☐	1	tablespoon cider vinegar	_____
☐	½	teaspoon salt	_____
☐	½	teaspoon black pepper	_____

1. Combine barbecue sauce, molasses, brown sugar and vinegar in a bowl and mix thoroughly. Taste, adjust flavoring.

2. Spray grill grate with no-stick cooking spray. Prepare grill for low-indirect heat. Center a disposable aluminum drip pan on charcoal grate. Add water to pan and replenish when needed while cooking. Distribute heated charcoal around pan. Season ribs with salt and black pepper.

3. Place ribs on grill. Ribs should not be directly over coals. Cover and grill 3 – 4 hours until done. Turn ribs and brush frequently with sauce. Maintain grill temperature at 275°. Internal temperature of ribs should be at least 160°.

NOTES: Date: _____

RATE THIS RECIPE

○ ○ ○ ○ ○

CAJUN BARBECUED BABY BACK RIBS

Grill 3 – 4 Hours

		INGREDIENTS	SUBSTITUTIONS
☐	3 – 4	pounds baby back ribs (2 meaty racks)	
☐	2	tablespoons Worcestershire sauce	_____
☐	¾	cup brown sugar – packed	_____
☐	2	tablespoons Cajun seasoning	_____
☐	2	garlic cloves – minced	_____
☐	1	tablespoon paprika	_____
☐	½	teaspoon salt	_____
☐	1	tablespoon black pepper	_____

1. Brush ribs with Worcestershire sauce.

2. In a bowl, combine remaining ingredients and mix thoroughly. Massage ribs evenly with rub.

3. Spray grill grate with no-stick cooking spray. Prepare grill for low-indirect heat. Center a disposable aluminum drip pan on charcoal grate. Add water to pan and replenish when needed while cooking. Distribute heated charcoal around pan.

4. Place ribs on grill over coals and sear. Move ribs over drip pan. Grill ribs covered 3 – 4 hours until done. Maintain grill temperature at 275°. Internal temperature of ribs should be at least 160°.

NOTES: Date: _____

RATE THIS RECIPE
○ ○ ○ ○ ○

CHERRY BABY BACK RIBS

Marinate | Grill 3 – 4 Hours

		INGREDIENTS	SUBSTITUTIONS
☐	3 – 4	pounds baby back ribs (2 meaty racks)	
☐	1	cup cherry preserves	_____
☐	3	tablespoons maraschino cherry juice	_____
☐	8	scallions – thinly sliced	_____
☐	½	cup soy sauce	_____
☐	1	teaspoon ginger	_____
☐	1	teaspoon nutmeg	_____
☐	2	garlic cloves – minced	_____
☐	½	teaspoon allspice	_____
☐	2	tablespoons Dijon mustard	_____
☐	1½	tablespoons brown sugar	_____
☐	3	scallions – sliced (garnish)	_____
☐	10	maraschino cherries – sliced (garnish)	_____

1. Blend cherry preserves, maraschino cherry juice, scallions, soy sauce, ginger, nutmeg, garlic and allspice in a bowl. Mix thoroughly.

2. Cut racks into two or three rib sections and place in a jumbo re-sealable plastic bag. Add cherry mixture to bag. Seal bag and marinate in refrigerator 8 hours. Turn several times to coat thoroughly.

3. Place marinade from bag in a saucepan and bring to a boil. Add mustard and brown sugar. Boil until marinade is reduced and thickened. Set aside.

4. Spray grill grate with no-stick cooking spray. Prepare grill to low-indirect heat. Center a disposable aluminum drip pan on charcoal grate. Add water to pan and replenish when needed while cooking. Distribute heated charcoal around pan.

5. Remove ribs from bag and pat dry with paper towels. Place ribs on grill and cook covered 3 – 4 hours until done. Brush ribs frequently with marinade during last half hour of grilling. Internal temperature should be at least 160°. Maintain grill temperature at 275°. Garnish with scallions and maraschino cherries.

NOTES: Date: _____

RATE THIS RECIPE
○ ○ ○ ○ ○

CHILI POWDER BABY BACK RIBS

Grill 3 – 4 Hours

		INGREDIENTS	SUBSTITUTIONS
☐	3 – 4	pounds baby back ribs (2 meaty racks)	
☐	3	tablespoons chili powder	_____
☐	1	teaspoon hot pepper sauce	_____
☐	1	teaspoon black pepper	_____
☐	½	teaspoon salt	_____
☐	2	teaspoons Herb de Provence	_____
☐	½	teaspoon onion powder	_____
☐	3	garlic cloves – minced	_____
☐	1	teaspoon ginger powder	_____

1. In a bowl, blend together all ingredients except ribs. Massage ribs evenly with rub.

2. Spray grill grate with no-stick cooking spray. Prepare grill for low-indirect heat. Center a disposable aluminum drip pan on charcoal grate. Add water to pan and replenish when needed while cooking. Distribute heated charcoal around pan.

3. Place ribs on grill and cook covered 3 – 4 hours until done. Turn several times while cooking. Maintain grill temperature at 275°. Internal temperature of ribs should be at least 160°.

NOTES: Date: _____

RATE THIS RECIPE
○ ○ ○ ○ ○

The **CHERRY BABY BACK RIBS** recipe on page 32 is special to me. For one thing, I've always been fond of cherries. But this recipe is special because before I cooked it for the first time, I prepared the marinade over and over in my imagination, altering an ingredient amount here, adding a new ingredient there. I even upped the cherry ante by conceptually adding the cherry juice to the sauce and the sliced cherries as a garnish. I had Dickensian Great Expectations before I ever set flame to rib, and when I finally did prepare it, I was not disappointed!

CHILI SAUCE / COLA BABY BACK RIBS

Grill 3 - 4 Hours

		INGREDIENTS	SUBSTITUTIONS
☐	3 – 4	pounds baby back ribs (2 meaty racks)	
☐	½	cup brown sugar – packed	_____
☐	1	teaspoon black pepper	_____
☐	1	teaspoon salt	_____
☐	1	tablespoon chili powder	_____
☐	2	garlic cloves – minced	_____
☐	½	teaspoon onion powder	_____
☐	½	teaspoon cayenne pepper	_____
☐	1	bottle (12 ounce) chili sauce	_____
☐	1	can (12 ounce) cola	_____
☐	¼	cup Worcestershire sauce	_____
☐	¼	cup steak sauce	_____
☐	¼	teaspoon liquid smoke	_____
☐	2	cups hickory wood chips – divided	_____

1. In a bowl, mix brown sugar, black pepper, salt, chili powder, garlic, onion powder and cayenne pepper. Massage ribs evenly with rub.

2. Combine chili sauce, cola, Worcestershire, steak sauce and liquid smoke in a saucepan and simmer 5 minutes. Divide into two bowls.

3. Spray grill grate with no-stick cooking spray. Prepare grill for low-indirect heat. Center a disposable aluminum drip pan on charcoal grate. Add water to pan and replenish when needed while cooking. Distribute heated charcoal around pan. Sprinkle 1½ cups of hickory chips over coals.

4. Sear ribs on meat side over coals and then place ribs bone-side down over drip pan. Cover and grill 1 hour. Sprinkle remaining hickory chips on coals. Maintain grill temperature at 275°. Baste ribs with sauce from one bowl. Cover and continue grilling ribs 2½ – 3½ hours until done. Internal temperature of ribs should be at least 160°.

5. Serve with remaining bowl of sauce.

NOTES: Date: _____

RATE THIS RECIPE
○ ○ ○ ○ ○

FENNEL SEED BABY BACK RIBS
Grill 1.5 Hours

		INGREDIENTS	SUBSTITUTIONS
☐	3 – 4	pounds baby back ribs (2 meaty racks)	
☐	1½	tablespoons ground fennel seeds	_____
☐	1	tablespoon ground cumin	_____
☐	1	teaspoon ground coriander	_____
☐	1	teaspoon ground cardamom	_____
☐	1	teaspoon dry mustard	_____
☐	½	teaspoon ground cinnamon	_____
☐	½	teaspoon ground ginger	_____
☐	¼	teaspoon garlic powder	_____
☐	2	teaspoons brown sugar	_____

1. Combine all ingredients except ribs in a bowl and mix thoroughly. Massage ribs evenly with rub.

2. Spray grill grate with no-stick cooking spray. Prepare grill for low-direct heat. Place ribs meat side up on grill. Grill ribs covered about 1 – 1½ hours until done. Turn several times while cooking. Maintain grill temperature at 275°. Internal temperature of ribs should be at least 160°.

NOTES:

Date: _____

RATE THIS RECIPE
○ ○ ○ ○ ○

I find shopping for ingredients to be a great deal of fun. I frequent many area grocery stores and meat markets, always searching for the freshest ingredients and the best bargains. Getting to know the wonderful people that staff these establishments has been a fantastic side benefit of my frequent visits.

For ingredients I use all the time, I purchase the largest amounts possible—large ketchup bottles, big jars of mustard, 64 ounce jugs of vinegar and enormous bottles of soy sauce. And I've learned that "on sale" ingredients, especially meats, are sometimes not the best they can be. Choose your ingredients carefully!

HICKORY CHIP BABY BACK RIBS
Grill 1 Hour | Oven 2 Hours

		INGREDIENTS	SUBSTITUTIONS
☐	3 – 4	pounds baby back ribs (2 meaty racks)	
☐	1	tablespoon dry mustard	_____
☐	1	tablespoon brown sugar	_____
☐	1	garlic clove – minced	_____
☐	½	teaspoon onion powder	_____
☐	1½	teaspoons celery salt	_____
☐	½	teaspoon cayenne pepper	_____
☐	½	teaspoon ground allspice	_____
☐	½	teaspoon ground ginger	_____
☐	1	cup hickory wood chips	_____
☐	1¼	cups ketchup	_____
☐	¼	cup molasses	_____
☐	¼	cup cider vinegar	_____
☐	¼	cup water	_____
☐	¼	teaspoon liquid smoke	_____

1. Combine mustard, brown sugar, garlic, onion powder, celery salt, cayenne pepper, allspice and ginger in a large bowl. Reserve 2 tablespoons. Massage remaining spice rub on to both sides of ribs.

2. Spray grill grate with no-stick cooking spray. Prepare grill for low-indirect heat. Center a disposable aluminum drip pan on charcoal grate. Add water to pan and replenish when needed while cooking. Distribute heated charcoal around pan. Scatter hickory chips over coals.

3. Place ribs on grill, cover and cook 1 hour turning ribs at least once. Maintain grill temperature at 275°. Leave cover slightly open to draw chip smoke up to ribs.

4. Place oven rack in middle position. Preheat oven to 250°. Place wire rack on rimmed baking sheet with enough water to cover sheet bottom. Place ribs on wire rack, cover securely with foil and cook 1½ – 2 hours in oven until done. Internal temperature of ribs should be at least 160°.

5. In a bowl, thoroughly blend reserved 2 tablespoons of rub, ketchup, molasses, vinegar, water and liquid smoke. Spoon sauce over ribs and serve.

NOTES: Date: _____

RATE THIS RECIPE
○ ○ ○ ○ ○

HOISIN SAUCE BABY BACK RIBS
Marinate | Grill 3 – 4 Hours

		INGREDIENTS	SUBSTITUTIONS
☐	3 – 4	pounds baby back ribs (2 meaty racks)	
☐	3	tablespoons honey	_____
☐	1	jar (8 ounce) hoisin sauce	_____
☐	1½	tablespoons soy sauce	_____
☐	1	tablespoon ketchup	_____
☐	2	teaspoons black bean sauce	_____
☐	1	teaspoon cider vinegar	_____
☐	½	teaspoon hot pepper sauce	_____
☐	¼	teaspoon liquid smoke	_____
☐	¼	teaspoon cayenne pepper	_____
☐	1	tablespoon ginger powder	_____
☐	¼	teaspoon onion powder	_____
☐	¼	teaspoon garlic powder	_____

1. Cut racks into two or three rib sections. Place in a jumbo re-sealable plastic bag.

2. In a large bowl, combine honey and hoisin sauce. Whisk in soy sauce. Add other ingredients to bowl and mix thoroughly. Taste, adjust flavoring. Add marinade to bag. Seal bag, place in refrigerator and marinate 8 hours. Turn occasionally to marinate thoroughly.

3. Spray grill grate with no-stick cooking spray. Prepare grill for low-indirect heat. Center a disposable aluminum drip pan on charcoal grate. Add water to pan and replenish when needed while cooking. Distribute heated charcoal around pan.

4. Remove ribs from bag and pour marinade from bag into a saucepan. Bring marinade to a boil, reduce heat and simmer 5 minutes.

5. Grill ribs covered 3 – 4 hours until done. Turn and baste ribs with marinade. Maintain grill temperature at 275°. Internal temperature of ribs should be at least 160°.

NOTES: Date: _____

RATE THIS RECIPE
○ ○ ○ ○ ○

HONEY / PLUM BABY BACK RIBS
Stove Top 15 Minutes | Grill 1.5 Hours

		INGREDIENTS	SUBSTITUTIONS
☐	3 – 4	pounds baby back ribs (2 meaty racks)	
☐	1	teaspoon dried oregano	_____
☐	¾	teaspoon dried thyme	_____
☐	2	garlic cloves – minced	_____
☐	½	teaspoon salt	_____
☐	1	teaspoon black pepper	_____
☐	2	tablespoons molasses	_____
☐	1	teaspoon dry mustard	_____
☐	2	tablespoons white wine	_____
☐	1	tablespoon Worcestershire sauce	_____
☐	¼	cup steak sauce	_____
☐	1	tablespoon soy sauce	_____
☐	½	teaspoon liquid smoke	_____
☐	2	tablespoons white vinegar	_____
☐	1	garlic clove – crushed	_____
☐	½	cup plum sauce	_____
☐	½	jar (6 ounce) honey	_____

1. Place ribs in a stockpot, cover with water and add oregano, thyme, garlic, salt and black pepper. Simmer 10 – 15 minutes.

2. Mix together all other ingredients and blend thoroughly to make basting sauce.

3. Spray grill grate with no-stick cooking spray. Prepare grill for low-direct heat. Transfer ribs from pot to grill and brush both sides of ribs with sauce. Grill ribs 1 – 1½ hours until done. Turn and baste with sauce several times. Maintain grill temperature at 275° while cooking. Internal temperature of ribs should be at least 160°.

NOTES: Date: _____

RATE THIS RECIPE
○ ○ ○ ○ ○

One of my great joys in creating this cookbook has been lavishing careful attention on the clarity of the step-by-step cooking instructions. Too many times I've attempted to prepare a "new-to-me" recipe and found that the instructions were confusing at best, and, at worst, downright detrimental to the finished product.

With this cookbook, every effort has been made to clearly document each step in the cooking process and to present those steps in a no-nonsense manner that facilitates a successful outcome.

Always read a recipe all the way through before beginning, confirming that it makes sense to you, and that you have the ingredients and cooking tools you'll need. I hope you agree that our persnickety emphasis on clarity has been worth the effort.

JALAPEÑO BABY BACK RIBS

Marinate | Grill 3 – 4 Hours

		INGREDIENTS	SUBSTITUTIONS
☐	3 – 4	pounds baby back ribs (2 meaty racks)	
☐	6	cups pineapple juice – divided	_____
☐	½	cup cilantro – chopped	_____
☐	2	jalapeño peppers – thinly sliced	_____
☐	½	cup cider vinegar	_____
☐	6	tablespoons brown sugar – divided	_____
☐	½	stick butter	_____
☐	2	teaspoons black pepper – divided	_____
☐	1	teaspoon salt	_____
☐	1½	teaspoons coriander	_____
☐	1	teaspoon ground cinnamon	_____
☐	1	teaspoon allspice	_____
☐	1	teaspoon cayenne pepper	_____

1. Place 4 cups pineapple juice, cilantro and jalapeños in a bowl and mix thoroughly. Cut racks into two or three rib sections. Place ribs in a re-sealable plastic bag. Add pineapple juice mixture, seal bag and refrigerate 8 hours. Turn bag occasionally to coat ribs evenly.

2. Combine remaining pineapple juice, vinegar, 3 tablespoons brown sugar, butter and 1 teaspoon black pepper in a large saucepan and bring to a boil over high heat. Reduce heat to medium and cook and stir until reduced to 1 cup. Set aside.

3. Dry ribs with paper towel. Combine 3 tablespoons brown sugar, 1 teaspoon black pepper, salt, coriander, cinnamon, allspice and cayenne pepper. Massage ribs evenly with spices.

4. Prepare grill for low-indirect heat. Lightly oil grill grates with no-stick cooking spray. Place ribs on grill, cover and grill for 3 - 4 hours until done. Brush with set aside pineapple/brown sugar glaze several times while grilling. Maintain grill temperature at 275°. Ribs are done when internal temperature has reached at least 160°.

NOTES: Date: _____

KETCHUP / ONION BABY BACK RIBS

Grill 3 – 4 Hours

		INGREDIENTS	SUBSTITUTIONS
☐	3 – 4	pounds baby back ribs (2 meaty racks)	
☐	2	teaspoons paprika	_____
☐	1	teaspoon salt	_____
☐	2	teaspoons black pepper	_____
☐	1	teaspoon cayenne pepper	_____
☐	1½	cups ketchup	_____
☐	1	large onion – chopped	_____
☐	¾	cup cider vinegar	_____
☐	½	tablespoon garlic powder	_____
☐	2	tablespoons Dijon mustard	_____
☐	½	cup brown sugar – packed	_____
☐	½	teaspoon hot pepper sauce	_____

1. Blend paprika, salt, black pepper and cayenne pepper thoroughly. Massage ribs evenly with rub.

2. Mix together remaining ingredients and blend thoroughly. Taste, adjust flavoring. Pour ingredients into a saucepan, bring to a boil, reduce heat and simmer 10 minutes. Set aside to cool.

3. Spray grill grate with no-stick cooking spray. Prepare grill for low-indirect heat. Center a disposable aluminum drip pan on charcoal grate. Add water to pan and replenish when needed while cooking. Distribute heated charcoal around pan. Place ribs on grill, cover and cook 3 – 4 hours until done. Maintain grill temperature at 275°. Baste frequently with sauce. Internal temperature of ribs should be at least 160°.

NOTES: Date: _____

RATE THIS RECIPE
○ ○ ○ ○ ○

It is simple to revise the flavor profile of a recipe by adding, removing or adjusting ingredients.

Experiment!

Always make adjustments and refinements to ingredients until the recipe is perfect for you.

KETCHUP / BROWN SUGAR BABY BACK RIBS

Grill 3– 4 Hours

		INGREDIENTS	SUBSTITUTIONS
☐	3 – 4	pounds baby back ribs (2 meaty racks)	
☐	¾	cup brown sugar – divided – packed	_____
☐	¼	cup paprika	_____
☐	1	tablespoon black pepper	_____
☐	1	tablespoon salt	_____
☐	1	tablespoon chili powder	_____
☐	1	garlic clove – minced	_____
☐	½	teaspoon onion powder	_____
☐	1	teaspoon cayenne pepper	_____
☐	3	tablespoons extra virgin olive oil	_____
☐	1	cup ketchup	_____
☐	¼	cup water	_____
☐	¼	cup vinegar	_____
☐	2	tablespoons paprika	_____
☐	1	tablespoon chili powder	_____

1. In a bowl, combine ½ cup brown sugar, paprika, black pepper, salt, chili powder, garlic, onion powder and cayenne pepper. Mix well. Massage ribs evenly with mixture.

2. Heat oil in a saucepan. Place all remaining ingredients except ribs in saucepan. Simmer ingredients about 15 minutes until thickened.

3. Spray grill grate with no-stick cooking spray. Prepare grill for low-indirect heat. Center a disposable aluminum drip pan on charcoal grate. Add water to pan and replenish when needed while cooking. Distribute heated charcoal around pan.

4. Place ribs on grill, cover and cook 3 – 4 hours until done. Turn occasionally. Brush with sauce often during cooking process. Maintain grill temperature between 275°. Internal temperature of ribs should be at least 160°.

NOTES: Date: _____

RATE THIS RECIPE
○ ○ ○ ○ ○

KETCHUP / ORANGE JUICE BABY BACK RIBS

Grill 3 – 4 Hours

		INGREDIENTS	SUBSTITUTIONS
☐	3 – 4	pounds baby back ribs (2 meaty racks)	
☐	1	cup ketchup	_____
☐	½	cup brown sugar – packed	_____
☐	½	cup orange juice concentrate – thawed	_____
☐	2	tablespoons cider vinegar	_____
☐	½	tablespoon ground ginger	_____
☐	1	tablespoon Dijon mustard	_____
☐	1	tablespoon Worcestershire sauce	_____
☐	½	teaspoon salt	_____
☐	½	teaspoon black pepper	_____

1. Add all ingredients except ribs in a bowl and blend thoroughly. Taste, adjust flavoring.

2. Spray grill grate with no-stick cooking spray. Prepare grill for low-indirect heat. Center a disposable aluminum drip pan on charcoal grate. Add water to pan and replenish when needed while cooking. Distribute heated charcoal around pan.

3. Place ribs on grill over drip pan and cook covered about 1 hour. Turn and brush with some sauce. Grill an additional 2½ – 3½ hours until done. Turn and baste ribs several times. Maintain grill temperature at 275°. Five minutes before removing ribs from grill, brush on a heavy coating of sauce. Internal temperature of ribs should be at least 160°.

NOTES: Date: _____

RATE THIS RECIPE
○ ○ ○ ○ ○

MAPLE SYRUP BABY BACK RIBS

Marinate | Grill 1.5 Hours

		INGREDIENTS	SUBSTITUTIONS
☐	3 – 4	pounds baby back ribs (2 meaty racks)	
☐	1	cup maple syrup	_____
☐	3	tablespoons cider vinegar	_____
☐	1	tablespoon soy sauce	_____
☐	½	teaspoon black pepper	_____
☐	½	teaspoon salt	_____

1. Combine syrup, vinegar and soy sauce in a small saucepan. Taste, adjust flavoring. Simmer 5 minutes. Reserve one third of sauce in a bowl and refrigerate.

2. Season ribs with salt and black pepper. Cut racks in half. Place ribs in a jumbo re-sealable plastic bag. Pour remaining sauce into bag. Seal bag, place in refrigerator and marinate 8 hours. Turn bag several times to thoroughly coat ribs.

3. Spray grill grate with no-stick cooking spray. Prepare grill for low-direct heat. Observe closely to prevent burning. Turn ribs and baste several times with refrigerated sauce while grilling. Grill ribs covered about 1 – 1½ hours until done. Maintain grill temperature at 275°. Internal temperature of ribs should be at least 160°.

NOTES: Date: _____

RATE THIS RECIPE
○ ○ ○ ○ ○

MUSTARD / PEACH BABY BACK RIBS

Marinate | Grill 3 – 4 Hours

	INGREDIENTS	SUBSTITUTIONS
☐ 3 – 4	pounds baby back ribs (2 meaty racks)	
☐ ¼	cup honey mustard	_____
☐ 4	tablespoons peach preserves	_____
☐ 2	tablespoons duck sauce	_____
☐ 3	tablespoons extra virgin olive oil	_____
☐ 2½	tablespoons lemon juice	_____
☐ 1	tablespoon paprika	_____
☐ ½	teaspoon garlic powder	_____
☐ 1	teaspoon ginger powder	_____
☐ ½	teaspoon salt	_____
☐ ½	teaspoon black pepper	_____

1. Combine all ingredients except ribs in a blender. Blend until thoroughly mixed. Taste, adjust flavoring. Divide marinade equally into two bowls. Reserve one bowl in refrigerator to use later. Place ribs in a jumbo re-sealable plastic bag. Pour one bowl of marinade into bag. Seal bag and marinate in refrigerator 8 hours. Turn bag several times to marinate evenly.

2. Spray grill grate with no-stick cooking spray. Prepare grill for low-indirect heat. Center a disposable aluminum drip pan on charcoal grate. Add water to pan and replenish when needed while cooking. Distribute heated charcoal around pan. Do not place ribs over heat.

3. Cover and grill ribs 3 – 4 hours until done. Maintain grill temperature at 275°. Turn ribs several times. Brush occasionally with half the remaining sauce from refrigerator. Internal temperature of ribs should be at least 160°.

NOTES: Date: _____

RATE THIS RECIPE

○ ○ ○ ○ ○

Rib racks may be cut into halves, quarters or individual ribs for convenient handling.

Use a meat thermometer and monitor the pork ribs carefully as they cook to ensure they reach an internal temperature of at least 160°.

MUSTARD / WHISKEY BABY BACK RIBS
Marinate | Grill 1 Hour

		INGREDIENTS	SUBSTITUTIONS
☐	3 – 4	pounds baby back ribs (2 meaty racks)	
☐	1	tablespoon extra virgin olive oil	_____
☐	1	small onion – chopped	_____
☐	2	garlic cloves – minced	_____
☐	1	cup brown sugar – packed	_____
☐	½	cup ketchup	_____
☐	¼	cup Dijon mustard	_____
☐	¼	cup water	_____
☐	¼	cup Worcestershire sauce	_____
☐	¼	cup cider vinegar	_____
☐	1	cup whiskey	_____
☐	1	tablespoon chili powder	_____
☐	1	tablespoon dry mustard	_____
☐	½	teaspoon cayenne pepper	_____
☐	1	teaspoon ground cinnamon	_____

1. Heat oil in a large stockpot over medium heat. Add onion and garlic and sauté until onion is wilted and translucent. Add brown sugar, ketchup, mustard, water, Worcestershire, vinegar and whiskey. Simmer mixture on low 1 hour stirring occasionally until thickened. Refrigerate.

2. Mix chili powder, mustard, cayenne pepper and cinnamon in medium bowl. Massage spice mixture evenly over both sides of ribs. Cut racks in half. Place ribs in a jumbo re-sealable plastic bag. Add excess rub to bag. Seal bag and refrigerate 8 hours. Turn bag several times to thoroughly coat ribs.

3. Spray grill grate with no-stick cooking spray. Prepare grill for low-direct heat. Arrange ribs on grill and grill about 25 minutes. Turn once. Cut racks into individual ribs. Arrange on baking sheet. Baste ribs with refrigerated sauce. Place sheet with ribs on grill and cook covered 30 – 40 minutes until done. Turn and baste ribs with sauce. Maintain grill temperature at 275° while cooking. Internal temperature of ribs should be at least 160°.

NOTES: Date: _____

RATE THIS RECIPE
○ ○ ○ ○ ○

ORANGE / APRICOT BABY BACK RIBS
Grill 3 – 4 Hours

		INGREDIENTS	SUBSTITUTIONS
☐	3 – 4	pounds baby back ribs (2 meaty racks)	
☐	1	cup orange marmalade	_____
☐	1	cup apricot jam	_____
☐	2	tablespoons sherry vinegar	_____
☐	⅓	cup cider vinegar	_____
☐	2	teaspoons ground cumin	_____
☐	1	teaspoon dried thyme	_____
☐	2	tablespoons chives – chopped (garnish)	_____

1. Combine all ingredients except ribs and chives in a bowl and blend thoroughly. Taste, adjust flavoring.

2. Spray grill grate with no-stick cooking spray. Prepare grill for low-indirect heat. Center a disposable aluminum drip pan on charcoal grate. Add water to pan and replenish when needed while cooking. Distribute heated charcoal around pan.

3. Place ribs on grill and grill covered 3 – 4 hours until done. Do not place ribs over coals. Turn and brush ribs with orange/apricot sauce several times. Maintain grill temperature at approximately 275°. Internal temperature of ribs should be at least 160°. Garnish with chives.

NOTES: Date: _____

RATE THIS RECIPE
○ ○ ○ ○ ○

ORANGE BABY BACK RIBS

Grill 3 – 4 Hours

		INGREDIENTS	SUBSTITUTIONS
☐	3 – 4	pounds baby back ribs (2 meaty racks)	
☐	½	cup orange marmalade	_____
☐	3	tablespoons soy sauce	_____
☐	2	tablespoons lemon juice	_____
☐	1	tablespoon Worcestershire sauce	_____
☐	¾	tablespoon ground ginger	_____
☐	½	teaspoon paprika	_____

1. Place all ingredients except ribs in a bowl and blend thoroughly. Taste, adjust flavoring.

2. Spray grill grate with no-stick cooking spray. Prepare grill for low-indirect grilling. Center a disposable aluminum drip pan on charcoal grate. Add water to pan and replenish when needed while cooking. Distribute heated charcoal around pan.

3. Place ribs on grill. Grill covered 3 – 4 hours until done. Do not place ribs over coals. Turn and brush ribs heavily with sauce several times. Maintain grill temperature at approximately 275°. Internal temperature of ribs should be at least 160°.

4. Brush ribs with any remaining sauce before serving.

NOTES: Date: _____

RATE THIS RECIPE
○ ○ ○ ○ ○

ORANGE JUICE / CHILI BABY BACK RIBS

Marinate | Grill 3 – 4 Hours

	INGREDIENTS	SUBSTITUTIONS
☐	3 – 4 pounds baby back ribs (2 meaty racks)	
☐	1½ cups orange juice	_____
☐	½ cup chili sauce	_____
☐	2 tablespoons duck sauce	_____
☐	1 tablespoon hoisin sauce	_____
☐	2 tablespoons brown sugar	_____
☐	2 garlic cloves – minced	_____
☐	½ teaspoon ground ginger	_____
☐	½ teaspoon onion powder	_____
☐	3 green onions – chopped (garnish)	_____

1. Cut racks into two or three rib sections and place in a jumbo re-sealable plastic bag. Add orange juice to bag, seal and marinate in refrigerator 8 hours.

2. Blend chili sauce, duck sauce, hoisin sauce, brown sugar, garlic, ginger and onion powder in a bowl. Taste, adjust flavoring. Set aside.

3. Spray grill grate with no-stick cooking spray. Prepare grill for low-indirect heat. Center a disposable aluminum drip pan on charcoal grate. Add water to pan and replenish when needed while cooking. Distribute heated charcoal around pan.

4. Remove ribs from bag and pat dry with paper towels. Place ribs on grill and cook 3 – 4 hours until done. Maintain grill temperature at 275°. Brush frequently with set aside sauce during last half hour of grilling. Ribs are done when internal temperature has reached at least 160°. Garnish with green onions.

NOTES: Date: _____

RATE THIS RECIPE
○ ○ ○ ○ ○

ORANGE JUICE / HERB BABY BACK RIBS
Grill 1.5 Hours

		INGREDIENTS	SUBSTITUTIONS
☐	3 – 4	pounds baby back ribs (2 meaty racks)	
☐	1	cup orange juice	_____
☐	2	garlic cloves – minced	_____
☐	1	teaspoon ginger powder	_____
☐	1	cup tomato sauce	_____
☐	¼	cup honey	_____
☐	1	teaspoon dry mustard	_____
☐	1	teaspoon jalapeño pepper – seeded/finely chopped	_____
☐	½	teaspoon rosemary	_____
☐	½	teaspoon oregano	_____
☐	½	teaspoon thyme	_____
☐	½	teaspoon salt	_____
☐	½	teaspoon black pepper	_____

1. Cut rib racks in half. Place ribs in a large stockpot, cover with water and bring to a boil. Reduce heat and simmer 10 minutes.

2. Place all ingredients except ribs in another saucepan and simmer 5 minutes. Taste, adjust flavoring.

3. Spray grill grate with no-stick cooking spray. Prepare grill for low-direct heat. Baste ribs with sauce and place on grill. Cook covered about 1 – 1½ hours, basting and turning ribs occasionally until done. Maintain grill temperature at 275°. Internal temperature of ribs should be at least 160°.

NOTES: Date: _____

RATE THIS RECIPE
○ ○ ○ ○ ○

PEANUT BUTTER BABY BACK RIBS

Marinate | Grill 1.5 Hours

	INGREDIENTS	SUBSTITUTIONS
☐ 3 – 4	pounds baby back ribs (2 meaty racks)	
☐ 6	scallions – sliced	_____
☐ ¾	cup soy sauce	_____
☐ ¼	cup sesame oil	_____
☐ ½	cup rice wine	_____
☐ 5	tablespoons peanut butter	_____
☐ ¼	cup brown sugar – packed	_____
☐ 1	tablespoon curry powder	_____
☐ ½	teaspoon black pepper	_____
☐ ½	teaspoon garlic powder	_____
☐ ½	tablespoon ground ginger	_____

1. Combine all ingredients except ribs in a blender. Blend until thoroughly mixed. Taste, adjust flavoring.

2. Divide marinade equally into two bowls. Reserve one bowl in refrigerator to use later while grilling.

3. Place ribs in a jumbo re-sealable plastic bag. Pour 1 bowl of marinade into bag. Seal bag and marinate in refrigerator 8 hours. Turn bag several times to marinate evenly.

4. Spray grill grate with no-stick cooking spray. Prepare grill for low-direct heat. Grill ribs covered about 1 – 1½ hours until done. Maintain grill temperature at 275°. Turn ribs several times. Brush occasionally with reserved sauce while cooking. Internal temperature of ribs should be at least 160°.

NOTES: Date: _____

RATE THIS RECIPE
○ ○ ○ ○ ○

Protect yourself when working with peppers. Use eye protection and rubber or latex gloves. Wash your hands thoroughly with soap and warm water before touching your eyes, mouth and other sensitive areas.

PINEAPPLE SAUCE BABY BACK RIBS

Marinate | Grill 3 – 4 Hours

		INGREDIENTS	SUBSTITUTIONS
☐	3 – 4	pounds baby back ribs (2 meaty racks)	
☐	½	teaspoon salt	_____
☐	3	tablespoons brown sugar – packed	_____
☐	½	teaspoon garlic powder	_____
☐	½	teaspoon ground ginger	_____
☐	2	teaspoons fresh thyme	_____
☐	3	tablespoons chili powder	_____
☐	¼	teaspoon black pepper	_____
☐	¼	teaspoon cayenne pepper	_____
☐	2½	cups pineapple juice	_____
☐	3	tablespoons ketchup	_____
☐	2	tablespoons Dijon mustard	_____
☐	1	tablespoon Worcestershire sauce	_____

1. Mix salt, brown sugar, garlic powder, ginger, thyme, chili powder, black pepper and cayenne pepper in a bowl. Rub spice mixture evenly over ribs.

2. Put ribs into a jumbo re-sealable plastic bag. Seal and marinate in refrigerator 8 hours. Turn occasionally to coat ribs evenly.

3. Combine pineapple juice, ketchup, mustard and Worcestershire in a saucepan over medium heat. Simmer until reduced to about 2 cups, approximately 20 – 30 minutes. Cover and set aside.

4. Spray grill grate with no-stick cooking spray. Prepare grill for low-indirect heat. Center a disposable aluminum drip pan on charcoal grate. Add water to pan and replenish when needed while cooking. Distribute heated charcoal around pan. Ribs should not be directly over heat.

5. Grill covered 3 – 4 hours until done. Maintain grill temperature at 275°. Baste three or four times with pineapple sauce during last half hour of cooking. Internal temperature of ribs should be at least 160°.

NOTES: Date: _____

RATE THIS RECIPE
○ ○ ○ ○ ○

ROOT BEER BARBECUED BABY BACK RIBS

Grill 1.5 Hours

		INGREDIENTS	SUBSTITUTIONS
☐	3 – 4	pounds baby back ribs (2 meaty racks))	
☐	4	tablespoons lemon juice	_____
☐	2	teaspoons hot pepper sauce	_____
☐	1	garlic clove – minced	_____
☐	1	tablespoon cider vinegar	_____
☐	½	medium onion – diced	_____
☐	1	cup root beer	_____
☐	¼	teaspoon liquid smoke	_____
☐	¾	cup ketchup	_____
☐	¼	teaspoon black pepper	_____
☐	3	tablespoons Worcestershire sauce	_____
☐	½	teaspoon salt	_____
☐	2	tablespoons steak sauce	_____

1. In a saucepan, combine all ingredients except ribs. Bring to a boil. Reduce heat and simmer sauce until thickened, about 10 – 15 minutes. Taste, adjust flavoring. Remove from heat and strain sauce through a fine mesh screen. Divide equally into two bowls. Reserve one bowl in refrigerator.

2. Spray grill grate with no-stick cooking spray. Prepare grill for low-direct heat. Place ribs on grill and cook covered about 1 – 1½ hours until done. Turn ribs and baste several times with sauce from one bowl while grilling. Maintain grill temperature at 275°. Internal temperature of ribs should be at least 160°.

3. Serve ribs with refrigerated bowl of sauce.

NOTES: Date: _____

RATE THIS RECIPE
○ ○ ○ ○ ○

SOY SAUCE BARBECUE BABY BACK RIBS

Marinate | Grill 3 – 4 Hours

		INGREDIENTS	SUBSTITUTIONS
☐	3 – 4	pounds baby back ribs (2 meaty racks)	
☐	½	cup water	_____
☐	½	cup soy sauce	_____
☐	2	tablespoons lemon juice	_____
☐	2	tablespoons extra virgin olive oil	_____
☐	1	tablespoon brown sugar	_____
☐	1	garlic clove – minced	_____
☐	1	teaspoon cider vinegar	_____
☐	1	teaspoon black pepper	_____
☐	½	teaspoon ginger	_____

1. In a bowl, combine all ingredients except ribs and mix thoroughly. Taste, adjust flavoring. Divide sauce equally between two bowls. Reserve one bowl in refrigerator. Add remaining bowl of mixture to a jumbo re-sealable plastic bag. Cut racks into two or three rib sections. Add ribs to bag. Seal bag and marinate in refrigerator 8 hours. Turn ribs several times while marinating to coat thoroughly.

2. Spray grill grate with no-stick cooking spray. Prepare grill for low-indirect heat. Center a disposable aluminum drip pan on charcoal grate. Add water to pan and replenish when needed while cooking. Distribute heated charcoal around pan.

3. Place ribs on grill, cover and cook 3 – 4 hours until done. Maintain temperature around 275°. Baste several times with reserved marinade. Internal temperature of ribs should be at least 160°.

NOTES: Date: _____

TOMATO SAUCE BABY BACK RIBS

Grill 3 – 4 Hours

		INGREDIENTS	SUBSTITUTIONS
☐	3 – 4	pounds baby back ribs (2 meaty racks)	
☐	½	stick butter	_____
☐	2	small onions – chopped	_____
☐	1	garlic clove – minced	_____
☐	1	can (15 ounce) tomato sauce	_____
☐	½	cup cider vinegar	_____
☐	½	cup brown sugar – packed	_____
☐	2	tablespoons chili powder	_____
☐	1	tablespoon Dijon mustard	_____
☐	½	teaspoon ginger – minced	_____
☐	½	teaspoon black pepper	_____

1. Melt butter in large saucepan. Add onions and garlic and sauté until onions are wilted and translucent. Add remaining ingredients except ribs. Bring to a boil stirring continually. Taste, adjust flavoring. Remove sauce from heat and cool.

2. Spray grill grate with no-stick cooking spray. Prepare grill for low-indirect heat. Center a disposable aluminum drip pan on charcoal grate. Add water to pan and replenish when needed while cooking. Distribute heated charcoal around pan.

3. Sear ribs over hot coals 1 – 2 minute on each side. Move ribs over drip pan and grill covered 3 – 4 hours until done. Baste with sauce during last 30 minutes of grilling. Maintain grill temperature at approximately 275°. Ribs are done when internal temperature has reached approximately 160°.

NOTES: Date: _____

VINEGAR / BROWN SUGAR BABY BACK RIBS
Grill 1.5 Hours

	INGREDIENTS	SUBSTITUTIONS
☐ 3 – 4	pounds baby back ribs (2 meaty racks)	
☐ ¼	stick butter	_____
☐ ¾	cup cider vinegar	_____
☐ ¼	cup brown sugar – packed	_____
☐ 1	tablespoon hot pepper flakes	_____
☐ 2	garlic cloves – minced	_____
☐ ½	teaspoon onion powder	_____
☐ ½	teaspoon salt	_____
☐ 1	teaspoon black pepper	_____

1. Melt butter in a saucepan over low heat. Add all ingredients except ribs, salt and black pepper. Simmer and stir frequently 10 minutes. Taste, adjust flavoring.

2. Spray grill grate with no-stick cooking spray. Prepare grill for low-direct heat.

3. Season ribs with salt and black pepper. Place ribs on grill. Brush with sauce, cover and grill about 1 – 1½ hour until done. Baste frequently with sauce. Maintain grill temperature at 275°. Internal temperature of ribs should be at least 160°.

4. Serve with remaining sauce.

NOTES:

Date: _____

RATE THIS RECIPE
○ ○ ○ ○ ○

A "trinity" is the combination of three essential ingredients as the flavoring base in a recipe, often created by sautéing a combination of any three aromatic vegetables, condiments, seasonings, herbs or spices. Geographic regions often have a trinity of ingredients that comprise the flavor base of dishes for that cuisine. If a recipe calls for a base of onion, bell pepper and celery, it is a good bet it is a Louisiana Creole dish. See Table 6 in the Appendix for a list of regional trinities.

If there is a trinity for barbecue sauces and glazes, it is vinegar, brown sugar/honey and a tomato base (ketchup, tomato paste, tomato purée or tomato soup). In these rib recipes you will find one, two or mostly likely all three of these components.

As you create your own rib sauces and marinades from a blank canvas, you can't go wrong by starting with the trinity base and working outward from there. Add soy sauce, Worcestershire sauce, garlic powder, onion powder or just about any other ingredient that you think might work to create a concoction that is wholly your own.

WHISKEY / APPLE CIDER BABY BACK RIBS

Marinate | Grill 3 – 4 Hours

		INGREDIENTS	SUBSTITUTIONS
☐	3 – 4	pounds baby back ribs (2 meaty racks)	
☐	½	cup whiskey	_____
☐	½	cup apple cider	_____
☐	2	tablespoons brown sugar	_____
☐	1	tablespoon Dijon mustard	_____
☐	¼	teaspoon cayenne pepper	_____
☐	½	teaspoon vanilla extract	_____
☐	4	teaspoons cider vinegar – divided	_____
☐	¼	teaspoon salt	_____
☐	¼	teaspoon black pepper	_____
☐	¼	stick butter	_____

1. Blend whiskey, cider, brown sugar, mustard, cayenne pepper, vanilla and 2 teaspoons vinegar together in a bowl. Taste, adjust flavoring. Pour half of mixture into a jumbo re-sealable plastic bags. Refrigerate remaining half of whiskey mixture.

2. Cut racks into two or three rib sections. Add ribs to bag. Seal bag, marinate and refrigerate 8 hours.

3. Spray grill grate with no-stick cooking spray. Prepare grill for low-indirect heat. Center a disposable aluminum drip pan on charcoal grate. Add water to pan and replenish when needed while cooking. Distribute heated charcoal around pan.

4. Pour refrigerated sauce into a large skillet and bring to a boil. Cook until thickened. Reduce heat and add remaining 2 teaspoons vinegar, salt, black pepper and butter. Simmer until thick.

5. Place ribs over drip pan. Grill ribs covered 3 – 4 hours until done. Turn frequently. Maintain grill temperature at 275°. Baste ribs several times with remaining sauce 20 minutes before end of grilling. Internal temperature of ribs should be at least 160°.

6. Spoon remaining sauce over ribs and serve.

NOTES: Date: _____

RATE THIS RECIPE
○ ○ ○ ○ ○

WHISKEY / KETCHUP BABY BACK RIBS

Grill 3 – 4 Hours

		INGREDIENTS	SUBSTITUTIONS
☐	3 – 4	pounds baby back ribs (2 meaty racks)	
☐	½	teaspoon salt	_____
☐	1	teaspoon black pepper	_____
☐	1½	cups ketchup	_____
☐	½	cup molasses	_____
☐	½	cup whiskey	_____
☐	¼	cup Dijon mustard	_____
☐	2	teaspoons hot pepper sauce	_____
☐	2	tablespoons Worcestershire sauce	_____
☐	2	teaspoons paprika	_____
☐	½	teaspoon garlic powder	_____
☐	½	teaspoon onion powder	_____

1. Combine all ingredients except ribs in a large saucepan. Bring to boil over medium heat stirring occasionally. Taste, adjust flavoring. Reduce heat to medium-low. Simmer uncovered stirring frequently until sauce thickens. Divide sauce equally into two bowls. Refrigerate one bowl.

2. Spray grill grate with no-stick cooking spray. Prepare grill for low-indirect heat. Center a disposable aluminum drip pan on charcoal grate. Add water to pan and replenish when needed while cooking. Distribute heated charcoal around pan.

3. Place ribs on grill and cover. Grill ribs 3 – 4 hours until done. Turn ribs and baste with one bowl of sauce several times while grilling. Maintain grill temperature at approximately 275°. Internal temperature of ribs should be at least 160°.

4. Serve with refrigerated bowl of whiskey sauce.

NOTES: Date: _____

RATE THIS RECIPE
○ ○ ○ ○ ○

OVEN COOKED
BABY BACK RIBS

Most fires are the result of unattended cooking. Keep a sharp eye on pots and pans, both on the stove top and in the oven.

Always, *always* have a properly rated fire extinguisher within arms reach. Familiarize yourself with the instructions and practice a dry-run so you can operate it if and when needed.

Never, *never* attempt to put out a grease fire with water. You will only cause the oil to erupt and this will spread the fire around the kitchen, and, in all probability, throughout the house.

BARBECUE SAUCE BABY BACK RIBS

Marinate | Oven 3 – 4 Hours

		INGREDIENTS	SUBSTITUTIONS
☐	3 – 4	pounds baby back ribs (2 meaty racks)	
☐	½	teaspoon cayenne pepper	_____
☐	½	teaspoon paprika	_____
☐	½	teaspoon onion salt	_____
☐	½	teaspoon black pepper	_____
☐	½	teaspoon white pepper	_____
☐	½	teaspoon salt	_____
☐	2	garlic cloves – minced	_____
☐	1½	tablespoons chili powder	_____
☐	1	tablespoon ground cumin	_____
☐	1	tablespoon celery salt	_____
☐	3	tablespoons white sugar	_____
☐	2	cups barbecue sauce	_____

1. In a large bowl, mix all ingredients except ribs and barbecue sauce together and mix well. Massage ribs evenly with rub.

2. Cut rib racks in half and place in a jumbo re-sealable plastic bag. Seal bag and marinate in refrigerator 8 hours.

3. Place oven rack in middle position. Preheat oven to 300°. Place ribs on a baking sheet. Cook covered 3 – 4 hours until done.

4. Brush ribs with barbecue sauce 10 – 15 minutes before ribs are done. Internal temperature of ribs should be at least 160°.

5. Cut ribs into individual pieces. Brush ribs with barbecue sauce before serving.

BELL PEPPERS BABY BACK RIBS

Oven 3 – 4 Hours

		INGREDIENTS	SUBSTITUTIONS
☐		3 – 4 pounds baby back ribs (2 meaty racks)	
☐	2	tablespoons hot pepper sauce	_____
☐	1	garlic clove – minced	_____
☐	1	tablespoon brown sugar	_____
☐	2	tablespoons black pepper	_____
☐	2	tablespoons seasoned salt	_____
☐	½	teaspoon curry powder	_____
☐	½	teaspoon chili powder	_____
☐	2	green bell peppers – seeded/julianne	_____
☐	2	red bell peppers – seeded/julianne	_____
☐	2	medium onions – sliced	_____

1. Combined hot pepper sauce, garlic, brown sugar, black pepper, seasoned salt, curry powder and chili powder in a bowl. Mix thoroughly. Massage ribs evenly with rub.

2. Place enough aluminum foil on a baking pan to wrap and seal ribs. Place 1 rib rack meat-side up on foil. Cover with half of bell peppers and half of onions. Place second rib rack on top and cover with remaining peppers and onions. Cut ribs to size if necessary but retain stacking technique. Wrap ribs with foil and seal tightly.

3. Move oven rack to middle position. Preheat oven to 300°. Bake ribs 3 – 4 hours until done. Ribs are done when internal temperature has reached at least 160°.

NOTES: Date: _____

BROWN SUGAR / PEPPERCORNS BABY BACK RIBS
Marinate | Oven 3 – 4 Hours

		INGREDIENTS	SUBSTITUTIONS
☐	3 – 4	pounds baby back ribs (2 meaty racks)	
☐	½	cup brown sugar – packed	_____
☐	½	cup extra virgin olive oil	_____
☐	¼	cup water	_____
☐	1½	tablespoons peppercorns	_____
☐	2	teaspoons duck sauce	_____
☐	½	tablespoon salt	_____
☐	2	teaspoons dried oregano	_____
☐	2	teaspoons dried rosemary	_____
☐	1	teaspoon cinnamon	_____
☐	1	tablespoon sesame seeds	_____
☐	2	teaspoons dried minced onion	_____

1. Combine all ingredients except ribs in a bowl and blend well to make marinade. Taste, adjust flavoring.

2. Cut rib racks in half. Place ribs in a jumbo re-sealable plastic bag. Add marinade, seal bag and refrigerator 8 hours. Turn occasionally while marinating to coat ribs evenly.

3. Place oven rack in top-third of oven. Place a baking pan of water on bottom rack of oven. Preheat oven to 300°. Lay ribs meat-side up on a rack in a shallow roasting pan. Pour marinade over ribs. Roast 3 – 4 hours basting ribs from time to time with pan juices until done. Internal temperature of ribs should be at least 160°.

NOTES: Date: _____

RATE THIS RECIPE
○ ○ ○ ○ ○

BROWN SUGAR / VINEGAR BABY BACK RIBS

Marinate | Oven 1 Hour | Quick Grill

		INGREDIENTS	SUBSTITUTIONS
☐	3 – 4	pounds baby back ribs (2 meaty racks)	
☐	3	garlic cloves – minced	_____
☐	½	teaspoon ground ginger	_____
☐	1	tablespoon rosemary – finely chopped	_____
☐	6	tablespoons brown sugar – divided	_____
☐	6	tablespoons cider vinegar – divided	_____
☐	½	teaspoon cayenne pepper	_____
☐	½	teaspoon salt	_____
☐	1	teaspoon black pepper	_____
☐	1½	cups water – divided	_____

1. Stir together garlic, ginger, rosemary, 1 tablespoon brown sugar, 1 tablespoon vinegar, cayenne pepper, salt and black pepper to create rub. Taste, adjust seasoning. Massage ribs evenly with rub and transfer to large roasting dish. Cover dish and marinate ribs in refrigerator 8 or more hours.

2. Place oven rack in middle position. Preheat oven to 400°. Pour ½ cup water into roasting dish with ribs. Cover dish with foil and seal tightly. Cook ribs 30 minutes. Turn ribs and cook uncovered additional 30 minutes. Remove dish from oven and transfer ribs to a platter.

3. Add 1 cup hot water to roasting dish and scrape up brown bits to make a glaze. Separate fat and discard. Transfer liquid to a large skillet. Add 5 tablespoons vinegar and 5 tablespoons brown sugar to skillet. Bring to a boil stirring occasionally. Simmer 15 minutes or until liquid is reduced to about three quarters of a cup.

4. Spray grill grate with no-stick cooking spray. Prepare grill for low-direct heat. Brush skillet mixture onto both sides of ribs. Grill ribs 15 – 20 minutes turning occasionally until done. Maintain grill temperature at 275°. Ribs are ready when internal temperature has reached 160°. Serve with remaining glaze.

NOTES: Date: _____

CITRUS BABY BACK RIBS

Marinate | Oven 4 – 6 Hours | Quick Broil

		INGREDIENTS	SUBSTITUTIONS
☐	3 – 4	pounds baby back ribs (2 meaty racks)	
☐	2	cups brown sugar – packed	_____
☐	2	tablespoons salt	_____
☐	1	teaspoon black pepper	_____
☐	1½	teaspoons garlic powder	_____
☐	3	teaspoons allspice	_____
☐	1	tablespoon lemon zest	_____
☐	1	tablespoon orange zest	_____
☐	2	cups pineapple juice – unsweetened	_____
☐	¼	cup lemon juice	_____
☐	¼	cup lime juice	_____
☐	¼	cup orange juice	_____
☐	¼	cup cider vinegar	_____
☐	1	orange – wedges (garnish)	_____

1. Combine brown sugar, salt, black pepper, garlic powder, allspice and zests together and blend well. Massage ribs evenly with rub. Cut racks into two or three rib sections. Place ribs in a re-sealable plastic bag, add excess rub, seal and refrigerate 8 hours

2. Combine pineapple juice, other juices and vinegar in a large roasting pan. Add ribs. Cover tightly with aluminum foil. Move one oven rack to middle position and one oven rack to broil position. Preheat oven to 250°. Bake ribs 4 – 6 hours until done. Ribs are done when internal temperature has reached at least 160°. Remove from oven.

3. Drain braising liquid into large saucepan. Boil liquid 20 minutes until reduced by half. Stir occasionally.

4. Set oven to BROIL. Brush both sides of rib with sauce. Broil each side 3 – 4 minutes until browned. Garnish with orange wedges.

NOTES: Date: _____

RATE THIS RECIPE
○ ○ ○ ○ ○

CITRUS / MINT BABY BACK RIBS

Oven 3 – 4 Hours

		INGREDIENTS	SUBSTITUTIONS
☐		3 – 4 pounds baby back ribs (2 meaty racks)	
☐	2	tablespoons cornstarch	_____
☐	2	tablespoons brown sugar	_____
☐	1	tablespoon mint leaves – chopped	_____
☐	½	teaspoon salt	_____
☐	2	cups orange juice	_____
☐	2	tablespoons lime juice	_____
☐	1	teaspoon lime zest	_____
☐	2	teaspoons lemon zest	_____
☐	¼	teaspoon ginger – minced	_____
☐	1	orange – wedges (garnish)	_____

1. In a saucepan, combine cornstarch, brown sugar, mint and salt. Gradually stir in orange and lime juices. Stir and cook until thickened. Remove from heat and blend in lime zest, lemon zest and ginger. Taste, adjust flavoring.

2. Cut racks into two or three rib sections. Brush ribs liberally with sauce. Place oven rack in middle position. Preheat oven to 300°. Cover broiler pan with aluminum foil. Spray foil with no-stick cooking spray.

3. Place ribs on broiler pan and cover with foil. Bake 1½ – 2 hours. Baste ribs with occasionally with sauce. Bake an additional 1½ – 2 hours until done. Ribs are done when internal temperature has reached at least 160°. Garnish with orange wedges.

NOTES: Date: _____

RATE THIS RECIPE
○ ○ ○ ○ ○

CITRUS / SOY SAUCE BABY BACK RIBS

Marinate | Oven 3 – 4 Hours

		INGREDIENTS	SUBSTITUTIONS
☐	3 – 4	pounds baby back ribs (2 meaty racks)	
☐	¼	cup orange juice	_____
☐	2	tablespoons duck sauce	_____
☐	¼	cup soy sauce	_____
☐	¼	cup brown sugar – packed	_____
☐	1	teaspoon ground cumin	_____
☐	½	teaspoon ground ginger	_____
☐	½	teaspoon black pepper	_____
☐	3	green onions – chopped (garnish)	_____

1. Cut racks into individual ribs. Place ribs in a jumbo re-sealable plastic bags.

2. Stir together all ingredients except ribs and onions in a bowl until brown sugar is dissolved. Taste, adjust flavoring. Pour marinade into plastic bag. Seal bag and marinate ribs in refrigerator 8 hours. Turn bag several times while marinating to coat ribs thoroughly.

3. Put oven rack in middle position. Place pan of water on bottom oven rack. Preheat oven to 300°. Place ribs and marinade in a large baking dish. Place ribs meat-side down in baking dish with space between ribs. Roast ribs 1 hour, turn ribs and continue roasting additional 2 – 3 hours until ribs are done. Marinade should be thick and syrupy. Internal temperature of ribs should be at least 160°. Garnish with green onions.

NOTES: Date: _____

RATE THIS RECIPE
○ ○ ○ ○ ○

COLA / HABAÑERA BABY BACK RIBS
Oven 1 Hour | Quick Broil

		INGREDIENTS	SUBSTITUTIONS
☐	3 – 4	pounds baby back ribs (2 meaty racks)	
☐	1	cup cola	_____
☐	¼	cup cider vinegar	_____
☐	1½	cups brown sugar – packed	_____
☐	2	habañero chilies – seeded/finely chopped	_____
☐	½	teaspoon salt	_____
☐	1	teaspoon black pepper	_____

1. In a small saucepan, combine cola, vinegar, brown sugar and chilies. Bring to a boil over high heat. Reduce heat to medium-low and simmer until mixture is syrupy. Taste, adjust flavoring. Reduce heat to low and keep sauce warm while ribs cook.

2. Place one oven rack in middle position. Place another oven rack in broil position. Preheat oven to 300°. Season both sides of ribs with salt and black pepper. Line a baking sheet with aluminum foil. Spray foil with no-stick cooking spray.

3. Place ribs on foil and bake on middle oven rack 45 minutes basting ribs occasionally with cola sauce. Turn ribs and continue to cook additional 45 minutes. Brush with sauce occasionally.

4. Set oven to BROIL. Liberally spoon remaining sauce over ribs and broil meat side up 4 – 6 minutes until ribs are done. Internal temperature of ribs should be at least 160°.

NOTES: Date: _____

RATE THIS RECIPE
○ ○ ○ ○ ○

CRANBERRY GLAZED BABY BACK RIBS
Oven 2 Hours | Quick Broil

		INGREDIENTS	SUBSTITUTIONS
☐	3 – 4	pounds baby back ribs (2 meaty racks)	
☐	1	can (14 ounce) jellied cranberry sauce	_____
☐	½	cup water	_____
☐	¼	cup soy sauce	_____
☐	2	tablespoons Dijon mustard	_____
☐	3	tablespoons brown sugar	_____
☐	½	tablespoon ground ginger	_____
☐	1	teaspoon salt	_____
☐	1	teaspoon black pepper	_____

1. In a medium saucepan, melt jellied cranberry sauce with water over medium-high heat. Whisk in soy sauce, Dijon mustard, brown sugar and ginger. Reduce heat and simmer 10 minutes. Taste, adjust flavoring. Divide sauce equally into two bowls.

2. Place one oven rack in middle position. Place another oven rack in broil position. Preheat oven to 325°. Cover a large rimmed baking sheet with aluminum foil. Spray foil with no-stick cooking spray.

3. Place ribs bone side down on foil. Season ribs with salt and black pepper. Distribute one bowl of cranberry sauce over ribs. Seal ribs loosely with foil wrap and place on sheet. Bake 1½ – 2 hours. Unwrap ribs, turn ribs and baste with remaining half bowl of sauce.

4. Move oven rack to top rack. Set oven to BROIL. Broil ribs meat-side up 4 – 6 minutes until done. Internal temperature of ribs should be at least 160°.

NOTES: Date: _____

RATE THIS RECIPE
○ ○ ○ ○ ○

KETCHUP / VINEGAR BABY BACK RIBS
Oven 1.5 Hours

		INGREDIENTS	SUBSTITUTIONS
☐	3 – 4	pounds baby back ribs (2 meaty racks)	
☐	¾	cup ketchup	_____
☐	¼	cup cider vinegar	_____
☐	3	tablespoons Worcestershire sauce	_____
☐	3	tablespoons brown sugar	_____
☐	½	teaspoon salt	_____
☐	½	teaspoon liquid smoke	_____

1. Blend ketchup, vinegar, Worcestershire, brown sugar, salt and liquid smoke in a saucepan. Taste, adjust flavoring. Bring to a simmer over medium heat. Reduce heat to low and simmer uncovered about 30 minutes. Stir frequently until mixture thickens. Divide equally into two bowls.

2. Place oven rack in middle position. Preheat oven to 350°. Line a baking sheet with aluminum foil. Spray foil with no-stick cooking spray.

3. Place ribs bone-side down on foil. Brush ribs with one bowl of sauce. Bake 30 minutes. Turn ribs and baste with remaining bowl of sauce. Cook additional 50 – 60 minutes until done. Internal temperature of ribs should be at least 160°.

NOTES: Date: _____

RATE THIS RECIPE
○ ○ ○ ○ ○

The **THAI BARBECUED BABY BACK RIBS** recipe on page 104 is the only recipe in this rib collection that has fish sauce as an ingredient. As I tailor recipes to my own tastes, I remove fish sauce and substituted different ingredients. To put it bluntly, I don't care for fish sauce – at all. I know it is a primary flavoring ingredient in a good chunk of the world's cuisine, but it is an acquired taste that I have yet to acquire.

There are many people, however, who really like fish sauce. One of my sons had the temerity to tell me that it is delicious. Go figure. I've left the fish sauce in this one recipe to remind me that it is a viable flavoring ingredient. If you are one of those folk who enjoy fish sauce, don't hesitate to add it wherever and whenever you'd like.

KETCHUP / WHITE SUGAR BABY BACK RIBS

Marinate | Oven 2 Hours | Grill 30 Minutes

		INGREDIENTS	SUBSTITUTIONS
☐	3 – 4	pounds baby back ribs (2 meaty racks)	
☐	1	cup white sugar	_____
☐	1	teaspoon salt – divided	_____
☐	1	tablespoon black pepper – divided	_____
☐	2	tablespoons paprika	_____
☐	1	teaspoon cayenne pepper – divided	_____
☐	3	garlic cloves – minced	_____
☐	1	medium onion – chopped	_____
☐	2½	cups ketchup	_____
☐	1	cup hot water	_____
☐	3	tablespoons brown sugar	_____

1. In a medium bowl, mix together white sugar, ½ teaspoon salt, ½ tablespoon black pepper, paprika, ½ teaspoon cayenne pepper and garlic. Taste, adjust flavoring. Massage ribs liberally with mixture. Put ribs into a jumbo re-sealable plastic bag. Add any excess rub to bag. Seal bag and refrigerate 8 hours.

2. Place oven rack in middle position. Preheat oven to 250°. Bake ribs uncovered in a large roasting pan 2 hours until tender.

3. Take 6 tablespoons of drippings from roasting pan and place in a skillet over medium heat. Sauté onion until wilted and translucent. Stir in ketchup and simmer 4 minutes stirring constantly. Add ½ teaspoon salt, ½ tablespoon black pepper, ½ teaspoon cayenne pepper, water and brown sugar. Taste, adjust flavoring. Cover mixture and simmer on low about 1 hour until thickened. Stir frequently.

4. Spray grill grate with no-stick cooking spray. Prepare grill for low-direct heat. Cook ribs 20 – 30 minutes turning occasionally until done. Baste ribs with sauce during last 10 minutes of grilling. Maintain grill temperature at 275°. Internal temperature of ribs should be at least 160°.

NOTES: Date: _____

RATE THIS RECIPE
○ ○ ○ ○ ○

MOLASSES / HOISIN SAUCE BABY BACK RIBS

Oven 1 Hour | Grill 1.5 Hours

		INGREDIENTS	SUBSTITUTIONS
☐	3 – 4	pounds baby back ribs (2 meaty racks)	
☐	5	teaspoons molasses	_____
☐	2	garlic cloves – minced	_____
☐	½	teaspoon onion powder	_____
☐	3½	teaspoons Worcestershire sauce – divided	_____
☐	¼	cup soy sauce	_____
☐	¼	cup rice vinegar	_____
☐	¼	cup hoisin sauce	_____
☐	¼	cup ketchup	_____
☐	1½	teaspoons lemon juice	_____
☐	1½	teaspoons Dijon mustard	_____
☐	½	teaspoon ground ginger	_____

1. Combine molasses, garlic, onion powder and 2 teaspoons Worcestershire in a bowl and mix thoroughly.

2. Place oven rack in middle position. Preheat oven to 300°. Place small pan of water on bottom oven rack. Place ribs in a large baking pan. Brush sauce over ribs. Cover ribs and bake 1½ hours.

3. Combine soy sauce, vinegar, hoisin, ketchup, lemon juice, mustard, 1½ teaspoons Worcestershire and ginger in a saucepan. Bring to a boil and simmer uncovered 8 – 10 minutes until slightly reduced. Taste, adjust flavoring. Divide into two bowls.

4. Spray grill grate with no-stick cooking spray. Prepare grill for low-direct heat. Use sauce from one bowl and baste ribs. Grill ribs 15 – 25 minutes turning frequently until done. Maintain grill temperature at 275° while cooking. Internal temperature of ribs should be at least 160°.

5. Serve with remaining bowl of sauce.

NOTES: Date: _____

RATE THIS RECIPE
○ ○ ○ ○ ○

OYSTER SAUCE / HOISIN SAUCE BABY BACK RIBS

Marinate | Oven 3 Hours

		INGREDIENTS	SUBSTITUTIONS
☐	3 – 4	pounds baby back ribs (2 meaty racks)	
☐	¼	cup oyster sauce	_____
☐	¼	cup hoisin sauce	_____
☐	¼	cup soy sauce	_____
☐	¼	cup honey	_____
☐	2	tablespoons brown sauce	_____
☐	2	tablespoons sweet sherry	_____
☐	1	tablespoon ground ginger	_____
☐	2	garlic cloves – minced	_____
☐	2	teaspoons peanut oil	_____

1. Combine all ingredients except ribs in a bowl and blend well to make marinade. Taste, adjust flavoring.

2. Cut rib racks in half. Place ribs in a jumbo re-sealable plastic bag. Add marinade, seal bag and refrigerator 8 or more hours. Turn occasionally while marinating to coat ribs evenly.

3. Place oven rack in top third of oven. Preheat oven to 325°. Place a baking pan of water on an oven rack in lower third of oven. Lay ribs meat-side up on a rack in a shallow roasting pan. Roast 2 – 3 hours basting ribs frequently with pan juices until done. Ribs are ready when internal temperature has reached at least 160°.

NOTES: Date: _____

RATE THIS RECIPE
○ ○ ○ ○ ○

PLUM ROASTED BABY BACK RIBS
Oven 1.5 Hours

	INGREDIENTS	SUBSTITUTIONS
☐ 3 – 4	pounds baby back ribs (2 meaty racks)	
☐ 2	tablespoons soy sauce	_____
☐ ½	cup plum preserves	_____
☐ 1	tablespoon cider vinegar	_____
☐ ½	tablespoon ground ginger	_____

1. Combine soy sauce, plum preserves, vinegar and ginger in a bowl and mix thoroughly. Taste, adjust flavoring. Divide sauce equally between two bowls. Reserve and refrigerate one bowl. Brush both sides of ribs with sauce from second bowl.

2. Place ribs on a large, shallow foil-lined baking pan. Spray baking pan with no-stick cooking spray. Place oven rack in middle position. Preheat oven to 325°. Place ribs meat-side down, cover pan tightly with foil and bake ribs in oven 1 hour. Remove ribs from oven and turn ribs.

3. Increase oven temperature to 375°. Brush ribs with remaining refrigerated plum sauce and bake additional 30 – 40 minutes until done. Internal temperature of ribs should be at least 160°.

NOTES: Date: _____

RATE THIS RECIPE
○ ○ ○ ○ ○

RASPBERRY GLAZED BABY BACK RIBS

Oven 4 Hours

		INGREDIENTS	SUBSTITUTIONS
☐	3 – 4	pounds baby back ribs (2 meaty racks)	
☐	¼	cup maple syrup	_____
☐	¼	cup brown sugar – packed	_____
☐	1½	tablespoons raspberry preserves	_____
☐	¼	cup apple cider	_____
☐	¼	teaspoon crushed red pepper	_____
☐	½	tablespoon salt	_____
☐	2	teaspoons black pepper	_____

1. In a bowl, mix together all ingredients except ribs and blend thoroughly until brown sugar is dissolved. Taste, adjust flavoring.

2. Cover a large rimmed baking sheet with aluminum foil. Spray foil with no-stick cooking spray.

3. Place oven rack in middle position. Preheat oven to 300°. Place ribs bone side down on foil and bake 1 hour. Brush both sides of rib racks with raspberry sauce and bake meat-side up additional 2 – 3 hours until done. Brush ribs with sauce several times while cooking. Internal temperature of ribs should be at least 160°.

4. Serve with remaining sauce.

NOTES: Date: _____

RATE THIS RECIPE

○ ○ ○ ○ ○

SPICED RUM BABY BACK RIBS

Marinate | Oven 1 Hour | Grill 1 Hour

		INGREDIENTS	SUBSTITUTIONS
☐	3 – 4	pounds baby back ribs (2 meaty racks)	
☐	1	cup brown sugar – packed	_____
☐	¼	cup ketchup	_____
☐	¼	cup soy sauce	_____
☐	¼	cup Worcestershire sauce	_____
☐	½	cup spiced rum	_____
☐	½	cup chili sauce	_____
☐	2	garlic cloves – minced	_____
☐	1	teaspoon dry mustard	_____
☐	¼	teaspoon black pepper	_____

1. Cut racks into two or three rib sections. Place oven rack in middle position. Preheat oven to 325°. Wrap ribs in a double thickness of aluminum foil and bake 1 hour. Remove from oven and cool.

2. In a large bowl, mix together all remaining ingredients. Taste, adjust flavoring. Put ribs into a jumbo re-sealable plastic bag and pour marinade into bag. Seal bag and marinate in refrigerator 8 or more hours. Turn several times to thoroughly marinate ribs.

3. Drain marinade into a saucepan and bring to a boil. Reduce heat and simmer for 5 minutes.

4. Spray grill grate with no-stick cooking spray. Prepare grill for low-direct heat. Place ribs on grill, cover and cook about 1 hour, turning and basting occasionally with marinade until done. Maintain grill temperature at 300°. Internal temperature of ribs should be at least 160°.

NOTES: Date: _____

RATE THIS RECIPE
○ ○ ○ ○ ○

TEA RUB BABY BACK RIBS

Oven 1.5 Hours

		INGREDIENTS	SUBSTITUTIONS
☐	3 – 4	pounds baby back ribs (2 meaty racks)	
☐	6	bags black tea – divided	_____
☐	½	cup brown sugar plus 2 tablespoons – packed	_____
☐	¼	teaspoon ground ginger	_____
☐	½	teaspoon salt	_____
☐	¼	teaspoon black pepper	_____
☐	¼	cup orange zest	_____
☐	2	cups water	_____
☐	¼	cup orange juice	_____

1. Empty tea from 3 bags into a bowl and mix tea with ½ cup brown sugar, ginger, salt, black pepper and orange zest.

2. Massage tea mixture into ribs. Place ribs meat-side up in a roasting pan.

3. Steep remaining 3 tea bags in 2 cups boiling water 5 minutes. Discard bags and stir in remaining 2 tablespoons brown sugar and orange juice. Pour mixture around ribs in pan.

4. Place oven rack in middle position. Preheat oven to 275°. Cover ribs in roasting pan with aluminum foil and cook 1 hour. Remove pan from oven. Pour pan liquid into a saucepan and simmer over low heat.

5. Increase oven temperature to 425°. Baste ribs with some simmering liquid and return ribs to oven and cook uncovered 20 – 30 minutes until done. Baste several times with simmering liquid. Internal temperature of ribs should be at least 160°.

6. Brush ribs with remaining liquid. Cut racks into individual ribs and serve.

NOTES: Date: _____

RATE THIS RECIPE
○ ○ ○ ○ ○

THAI BARBECUED BABY BACK RIBS
Marinate | Oven 3 Hours

✓		INGREDIENTS	SUBSTITUTIONS
☐	3 – 4	pounds baby back ribs (2 meaty racks)	
☐	2	stalks lemon grass – thinly sliced	_____
☐	1	teaspoon fish sauce	_____
☐	2	tablespoons peanut oil	_____
☐	2½	tablespoons soy sauce	_____
☐	2½	tablespoons lime juice	_____
☐	½	tablespoon garlic powder	_____
☐	¼	cup cilantro – no stems/chopped	_____
☐	½	tablespoon ground ginger	_____
☐	3	tablespoons white sugar	_____
☐	2	teaspoons sesame oil	_____

1. Remove outer leaves of lemon grass and slice grass thinly. Mix all ingredients except ribs together in a small bowl and blend well. Taste, adjust flavoring.

2. Cut rib racks in half and place in a jumbo re-sealable plastic bag. Add sauce to bag, seal and marinate in refrigerator 8 or more hours. Turn occasionally to coat thoroughly.

3. Remove ribs from marinade. Pour marinade into a saucepan. Bring marinade to a boil. Reduce heat and simmer 5 minutes.

4. Preheat oven to 325°. Place a baking pan half full of water on bottom oven rack. Place second oven rack in middle position of oven. Place ribs meat-side up on a rack in a shallow roasting pan. Bake ribs covered 2 – 3 hours until done. Brush ribs from time to time with marinade. Internal temperature of ribs should be at least 160°.

NOTES: Date: _____

RATE THIS RECIPE

○ ○ ○ ○ ○

TOMATO PASTE / BROWN SUGAR BABY BACK RIBS

Oven 2 Hours | Quick Grill

		INGREDIENTS	SUBSTITUTIONS
☐	3 – 4	pounds baby back ribs (2 meaty racks)	
☐	1½	cups water	_____
☐	1	cup white vinegar	_____
☐	1	can (6 ounce) tomato paste	_____
☐	1	tablespoon Dijon mustard	_____
☐	½	cup brown sugar – packed	_____
☐	1	teaspoon liquid smoke	_____
☐	1	teaspoon salt	_____
☐	½	teaspoon onion powder	_____
☐	¼	teaspoon garlic powder	_____

1. Combine all ingredients except ribs in a saucepan and cook over medium heat. Bring to a boil, reduce heat to simmer and cook 45 – 60 minutes until sauce is thick.

2. Move oven rack to middle position. Preheat oven to 300°. Cut racks into two or three rib sections. Center ribs meat side down on sufficient aluminum foil to wrap ribs completely after basting. Baste ribs liberally with sauce. Wrap ribs with foil and seal tightly. Place on baking sheet and cook 2 hours.

3. Prepare grill for medium-direct heat. Spray no-stick cooking spray on grill grates. Grill ribs 5 - 6 minutes on each side until done. Ribs are done when internal temperature has reached at least 160°. Brush with remaining sauce while grilling.

NOTES: Date: _____

RATE THIS RECIPE
○ ○ ○ ○ ○

WHISKEY BABY BACK RIBS

Oven 2 Hours | Grill 1 Hour

		INGREDIENTS	SUBSTITUTIONS
☐	3 – 4	pounds baby back ribs (2 meaty racks)	
☐	½	teaspoon salt	_____
☐	½	tablespoon black pepper	_____
☐	1	teaspoon cayenne pepper	_____
☐	2	tablespoons extra virgin olive oil	_____
☐	½	medium onion – chopped fine	_____
☐	1½	cups water	_____
☐	½	cup tomato paste	_____
☐	½	cup cider vinegar	_____
☐	½	cup brown sugar – packed	_____
☐	2½	tablespoons honey	_____
☐	2	tablespoons Worcestershire sauce	_____
☐	½	cup whiskey	_____
☐	2	garlic cloves – minced	_____
☐	½	teaspoon onion powder	_____
☐	1	tablespoon dark molasses	_____

1. Cut each rib rack in half. Sprinkle salt, black pepper and cayenne pepper over ribs.

2. Place oven rack in middle position. Preheat oven to 250°. Wrap each half rack in foil. Place racks on a baking sheet. Bake 2 hours.

3. Heat oil in a medium saucepan over medium heat. Sauté onion until wilted and translucent. Stir in water, tomato paste, vinegar, brown sugar, honey and Worcestershire. Blend thoroughly. Add whiskey, garlic, onion powder and molasses. Taste, adjust flavoring. Bring mixture to a boil. Reduce heat and simmer until sauce thickens.

4. Spray grill grate with no-stick cooking spray. Prepare grill for low-direct heat. Remove ribs from oven and let stand 10 minutes. Unwrap racks from foil and place racks on grill. Brush sauce on ribs and grill ribs 20 – 30 minutes on each side until done. Maintain grill temperature at 275° while cooking. Internal temperature of ribs should be at least 160°

NOTES: Date: _____

RATE THIS RECIPE
○ ○ ○ ○ ○

WHISKEY SWEET BABY BACK RIBS

Oven 2 Hours | Quick Grill

		INGREDIENTS	SUBSTITUTIONS
☐	3 – 4	pounds baby back ribs (2 meaty racks)	
☐	1	teaspoon black pepper	_____
☐	2	teaspoons salt – divided	_____
☐	2	tablespoons extra virgin olive oil	_____
☐	½	medium onion – minced	_____
☐	1	cup water	_____
☐	1	can (6 ounce) tomato paste	_____
☐	½	cup cider vinegar	_____
☐	½	cup brown sugar – packed	_____
☐	2	tablespoons honey	_____
☐	1	tablespoon Worcestershire sauce	_____
☐	1	teaspoon liquid smoke	_____
☐	¼	cup whiskey	_____
☐	¼	teaspoon garlic powder	_____

1. Cut racks into two or three rib sections. Season with black pepper and 1 teaspoon salt. Wrap ribs completely in aluminum foil. Place ribs on a broiler pan. Place oven rack in middle position. Preheat oven to 300°. Cook ribs 2 hours.

2. Pour oil in a large saucepan over medium-high heat and sauté onions until wilted and translucent. Add remaining ingredients, bring to a boil, reduce to simmer and cook 1 hour until sauce thickens. Set aside.

3. Prepare grill for medium-direct heat. Spray grill grate with no-stick cooking spray. Grill ribs on each side until done. Brush ribs liberally with sauce while grilling. Ribs are done when internal temperature has reached at least 160°.

NOTES: Date: _____

RATE THIS RECIPE
○ ○ ○ ○ ○

STOVE TOP
BABY BACK RIBS

CURRY / LIME JUICE BABY BACK RIBS
Stove Top 1 Hour

		INGREDIENTS	SUBSTITUTIONS
☐	3 – 4	pounds baby back ribs (2 meaty racks)	
☐	2	tablespoons red curry paste	_____
☐	2	cups water – divided	_____
☐	¼	cup brown sugar – packed	_____
☐	2	teaspoons ground turmeric	_____
☐	2	teaspoons ground ginger	_____
☐	2	teaspoons soy sauce	_____
☐	¼	cup shallots – sliced	_____
☐	2	garlic cloves – minced	_____
☐	½	cup lime juice	_____

1. Blend curry paste, ½ cup water and brown sugar thoroughly in a large stockpot.

2. Cut racks into individual ribs. Add ribs to stockpot. Cook over medium heat 15 minutes. Stir occasionally.

3. Add 1½ cups water, turmeric, ginger and soy sauce to stockpot and blend thoroughly. Bring to a boil and lower heat to simmer. Cook uncovered 30 – 40 minutes until ribs are tender.

4. Add shallots, garlic and lime juice. Continue cooking additional 10 – 15 minutes until all ingredients are blended and ribs are done. Taste, adjust flavoring. Internal temperature of ribs should be at least 160°.

5. Serve ribs with sauce.

NOTES: Date: _____

RATE THIS RECIPE
○ ○ ○ ○ ○

DUCK SAUCE BABY BACK RIBS

Stove Top 1 Hour

	INGREDIENTS	SUBSTITUTIONS
☐ 3 – 4	pounds baby back ribs (2 meaty racks)	
☐ 2	tablespoons extra virgin olive oil	_____
☐ ½	medium onion – diced	_____
☐ ½	medium green bell pepper – diced	_____
☐ 2	celery stalks – diced	_____
☐ 1	apple – cored/diced	_____
☐ ½	cup duck sauce	_____
☐ ½	teaspoon ground ginger	_____
☐ ½	teaspoon garlic powder	_____
☐ ½	teaspoon salt	_____
☐ ½	teaspoon black pepper	_____
☐ 3	green onions – chopped (garnish)	_____

1. Cut racks into individual ribs. Place oil in a large stockpot and cook ribs on medium-high heat until golden brown. Remove ribs from stockpot.

2. Add onions, bell pepper and celery to skillet. Sauté until onion is wilted and translucent.

3. Return ribs to stockpot. Reduce heat to low simmer. Add apple, duck sauce, ginger and garlic powder and blend thoroughly. Add salt and black pepper to taste.

4. Simmer about 1 hour until done. Internal temperature of ribs should be at least 160°.

5. Garnish with green onions. Serve with sauce.

NOTES: Date: _____

KETCHUP / SUGAR / VINEGAR BABY BACK RIBS
Stove Top 1 Hour

		INGREDIENTS	SUBSTITUTIONS
☐	3 – 4	pounds baby back ribs (2 meaty racks)	
☐	2	tablespoons extra virgin olive oil	_____
☐	½	cup ketchup	_____
☐	½	cup brown sugar – packed	_____
☐	½	cup cider vinegar	_____
☐	1	tablespoon Worcestershire sauce	_____
☐	1	tablespoon soy sauce	_____
☐	½	tablespoon mustard powder	_____
☐	½	teaspoon cayenne pepper	_____
☐	½	teaspoon black pepper	_____
☐	½	cup water	_____

1. Cut racks into two or three rib sections.

2. Heat oil in a large stockpot over medium-high heat until hot. Add ribs and cook turning occasionally until golden browned.

3. Add all other ingredients to stockpot and mix thoroughly. Cover and simmer on medium-low heat approximately 1 hour until ribs are done. Internal temperature of ribs should be at least 160°.

NOTES: Date: _____

RATE THIS RECIPE
○ ○ ○ ○ ○

KETCHUP / WORCESTERSHIRE BABY BACK RIBS
Stove Top 30 Minutes | Grill 30 Minutes

		INGREDIENTS	SUBSTITUTIONS
☐	3 – 4	pounds baby back ribs (2 meaty racks)	
☐	¼	teaspoon salt	_____
☐	¼	teaspoon black pepper	_____
☐	2	garlic cloves – minced	_____
☐	1	celery stalk – chopped	_____
☐	1	small onion – chopped	_____
☐	1	tablespoon liquid smoke	_____
☐	1	cup ketchup	_____
☐	¼	cup Worcestershire sauce	_____
☐	¼	cup lemon juice	_____
☐	1	teaspoon hot pepper sauce	_____
☐	½	teaspoon celery seed	_____

1. Cut racks into two or three rib sections. Place ribs in a large stockpot and cover with water. Add salt, black pepper, garlic, celery and onion. Bring to a boil, reduce heat and simmer 30 minutes until ribs are tender. Remove ribs to a pan, cover and refrigerate.

2. Combine remaining ingredients in a saucepan and bring to a near boil. Reduce heat and simmer 10 minutes.

3. Prepare grill for medium-high heat. Spray grill grate with no-stick cooking spray. Grill ribs 20 – 30 minutes brushing frequently with sauce until done. Ribs are done when internal temperature has reached at least 160°.

NOTES: Date: _____

RATE THIS RECIPE
○ ○ ○ ○ ○

Take recommendations about operating a safe kitchen seriously. During one particularly memorable visit with my son's family, I was using their open flame gas stove to cook for my grandchildren. I was wearing a robe with a fine nap, and as I was sautéing onions in a skillet, flames shot up the sleeve! I got the robe off quickly, bunched it in a pile on the floor and smothered the flames. I was lucky I wasn't seriously injured. Instead, I was just a bit chilly.

Also, I burned myself more than a couple of times by grabbing the handle of my cast-iron skillet after it had been in a hot oven. I learned, rather slowly, to make oven mitts my constant cooking companions. Learn from my mistakes and use those oven mitts! Stay safe. Nothing ruins a cooking adventure faster than a fire, a cut or a burn.

PLUM BABY BACK RIBS

Stove Top 30 Minutes | Quick Grill | Quick Oven

		INGREDIENTS	SUBSTITUTIONS
☐	3 – 4	pounds baby back ribs (2 meaty racks)	
☐	4	cups chicken broth	_____
☐	2	tablespoons ground ginger	_____
☐	2	teaspoons allspice – divided	_____
☐	¼	cup soy sauce plus 1 teaspoon	_____
☐	4	garlic cloves – crushed	_____
☐	1	cup duck sauce	_____
☐	1	cup hoisin sauce	_____
☐	2	teaspoons sesame oil	_____
☐	¼	teaspoon chili powder	_____
☐	2	teaspoons sesame seeds – toasted (garnish)	_____
☐	¼	cup chives – chopped (garnish)	_____

1. Place broth, ginger, 1 teaspoon allspice, ¼ cup soy sauce and garlic in a large stockpot and slowly bring to a simmer. Cut racks into two or three rib sections. Add ribs to stockpot. Simmer uncovered 30 minutes. Remove ribs and set aside to cool.

2. Separate fat from cooking liquid and discard. Boil liquid gently until reduced to 1 cup. Set aside.

3. In a bowl, combine 1 teaspoon soy sauce, garlic, duck sauce, hoisin sauce, sesame oil, chili powder and 1 teaspoon allspice. Blend thoroughly. Divide equally into two bowls.

4. Brush ribs liberally with 1 bowl of sauce. Prepare gill for medium-direct heat. Spray grill grate with no-stick cooking spray heat. Grill ribs 8 –10 minutes until sauce has caramelized slightly.

5. Cover broiler pan with aluminum foil. Spray foil with no-stick cooking spray. Place ribs on broiler pan and brush liberally with second bowl of sauce. Bake in 425° oven 10 – 12 minutes until sauce has caramelized and ribs are done. Ribs are done when internal temperature has reached at least 160°.

6. Heat liquid from Step 2 and pour over ribs. Sprinkle with toasted sesame seed and garnish with chives.

NOTES: Date: _____

RATE THIS RECIPE
○ ○ ○ ○ ○

SAUERKRAUT / BABY BACK RIBS

Oven 40 Minutes | Stove Top 2 Hours

		INGREDIENTS	SUBSTITUTIONS
☐	3 – 4	pounds baby back ribs (2 meaty racks)	
☐	3	tablespoons extra virgin olive oil	_____
☐	½	teaspoon salt	_____
☐	½	teaspoon black pepper	_____
☐	1	bag (32 ounce) sauerkraut	_____
☐	1	teaspoon caraway seeds – crushed	_____

1. Brush oil over all sides of ribs. Sprinkled ribs lightly with salt and black pepper. Cut rib racks in half.

2. Place oven rack in middle position. Preheat oven to 350°. Place ribs on a large baking sheet. Bake 30 – 40 minutes until ribs are golden brown on each side. Turn once while baking.

3. Remove ribs from baking sheet and place in a large roasting pan. Distribute sauerkraut evenly over ribs. Sprinkle crushed caraway seeds over sauerkraut. Simmer on low heat 1½ – 2 hours until ribs are done. Ribs are ready when internal temperature has reached at least 160°.

NOTES: Date: _____

RATE THIS RECIPE

○ ○ ○ ○ ○

NOTES

SLOW COOKER
BABY BACK RIBS

BARBECUE SAUCE / CHERRY BABY BACK RIBS
Slow Cooker 6 – 8 Hours

		INGREDIENTS	SUBSTITUTIONS
☐	3 – 4	pounds baby back ribs (2 meaty racks)	
☐	1	teaspoon salt	_____
☐	1	teaspoon black pepper	_____
☐	2½	cups barbecue sauce	_____
☐	1	cup cherry preserves	_____
☐	1	tablespoon Dijon mustard	_____
☐	1	teaspoon cider vinegar	_____
☐	1	garlic clove – minced	_____

1. Cut racks into two or three rib sections. Season ribs with salt and pepper. Place oven rack in middle position. Preheat oven to 350°. Line a baking sheet with aluminum foil and spray foil with no-stick cooking spray. Place ribs in on baking sheet and cook in oven 15 minutes. Turn over, and cook another 15 minutes.

2. Cut racks into individual ribs. Place ribs bone side up in a slow cooker.

3. Combine remaining ingredients in a large bowl and blend well. Taste, adjust flavoring. Pour over ribs. Toss ribs to coat evenly.

4. Cook on low 6 – 8 hours until ribs are done. Resist removing lid too often. Slow cooking requires internal heat and condensation. Internal temperature of ribs should be at least 160°.

5. Serve with remaining sauce from slow cooker.

NOTES: Date: _____

RATE THIS RECIPE
○ ○ ○ ○ ○

BARBECUE SAUCE / RED WINE BABY BACK RIBS

Slow Cooker 6 – 8 Hours

		INGREDIENTS	SUBSTITUTIONS
☐	3 – 4	pounds baby back ribs (2 meaty racks)	
☐	½	cup water – divided	_____
☐	½	cup barbecue sauce	_____
☐	½	cup red wine	_____
☐	2	tablespoons Worcestershire sauce	_____
☐	1	teaspoon hot pepper sauce	_____
☐	½	teaspoon salt	_____
☐	½	teaspoon black pepper	_____

1. Combine all ingredients except a quarter cup of water and ribs in a bowl and blend well. Taste, adjust flavoring.

2. Cut rib racks in half. Place ribs in slow cooker. Add a quarter cup water. Cook 1 hour on low.

3. Add sauce to slow cooker, cover and cook ribs approximately 5 – 7 hours on low until done. Resist removing lid too often. Slow cooking requires internal heat and condensation. Ribs are ready when internal temperature has reached at least 160°.

NOTES: _____ Date: _____

RATE THIS RECIPE
○ ○ ○ ○ ○

BROWN SUGAR / KETCHUP BABY BACK RIBS
Slow Cooker 6 – 8 Hours

		INGREDIENTS	SUBSTITUTIONS
☐	3 – 4	pounds baby back ribs (2 meaty racks)	
☐	½	cup brown sugar – packed	_____
☐	½	cup ketchup	_____
☐	¼	cup cider vinegar	_____
☐	1	tablespoon ground ginger	_____
☐	1	tablespoon dry mustard	_____
☐	½	teaspoon cayenne pepper	_____
☐	½	teaspoon hot pepper sauce	_____
☐	½	teaspoon salt	_____
☐	½	teaspoon black pepper	_____

1. Whisk together all ingredients except ribs in a slow cooker. Taste, adjust flavoring.

2. Cut ribs into single rib pieces. Add ribs to slow cooker in a single row bone-side up. Toss to coat ribs evenly. Cook on low 6 – 8 hours until done. Resist removing lid too often. Slow cooking requires internal heat and condensation. Ribs are ready when internal temperature has reached at least 160°.

NOTES: Date: _____

RATE THIS RECIPE
○ ○ ○ ○ ○

CAJUN BABY BACK RIBS

Slow Cooker 6 – 8 Hours

		INGREDIENTS	SUBSTITUTIONS
☐	3 – 4	pounds baby back ribs (2 meaty racks)	
☐	½	cup barbecue sauce	_____
☐	½	teaspoon salt	_____
☐	2	tablespoons Cajun seasoning	_____
☐	1	teaspoon black pepper	_____
☐	½	teaspoon cayenne pepper	_____
☐	½	teaspoon onion powder	_____
☐	2	garlic cloves – minced	_____
☐	1	teaspoon paprika	_____
☐	½	teaspoon hot pepper sauce	_____
☐	½	teaspoon Worcestershire sauce	_____

1. Combine all ingredients except ribs in a bowl and blend thoroughly. Taste, adjust flavoring.

2. Cut rib racks in half. Place ribs in slow cooker. Add sauce to slow cooker and toss ribs to coat thoroughly.

3. Cover and cook ribs 6 – 8 hours on low until done. Resist removing lid too often. Slow cooking requires internal heat and condensation. Internal temperature of ribs should be at least 160°.

NOTES: Date: _____

RATE THIS RECIPE
○ ○ ○ ○ ○

ONION / BARBECUE SAUCE BABY BACK RIBS

Oven Broil | Slow Cooker 6 – 8 Hours

	INGREDIENTS	SUBSTITUTIONS
☐ 3 – 4	pounds baby back ribs (2 meaty racks)	
☐ ½	teaspoon salt	_____
☐ ½	teaspoon black pepper	_____
☐ 1	large onion – sliced	_____
☐ 3	tablespoons water – divided	_____
☐ 1	teaspoon paprika	_____
☐ 1	bottle (18 ounce) barbecue sauce	_____

1. Set oven rack to broil position. Preheat oven broiler. Spray large baking sheet with no-stick cooking spray. Place ribs on baking sheet and season with salt and black pepper. Brown ribs under broiler about 3 – 5 minutes on each side.

2. Place sliced onions and 1 tablespoon water in slow cooker. Add ribs to slow cooker, cover and cook 3 hours on low.

3. In a bowl, combine paprika, 2 tablespoons water and barbecue sauce. Blend thoroughly. Add to slow cooker. Cover and continue cooking on low additional 3 – 4 hours until done. Resist removing lid too often. Slow cooking requires internal heat and condensation. Ribs are ready when internal temperature has reached at least 160°.

NOTES: Date: _____

RATE THIS RECIPE
○ ○ ○ ○ ○   **129**

ORANGE BABY BACK RIBS

Slow Cooker 6 – 8 Hours

		INGREDIENTS	SUBSTITUTIONS
☐	3 – 4	pounds baby back ribs (2 meaty racks)	
☐	1	teaspoon salt	_____
☐	1	teaspoon black pepper	_____
☐	¼	cup soy sauce	_____
☐	½	cup orange marmalade	_____
☐	2	tablespoons orange juice	_____
☐	1	tablespoon ketchup	_____
☐	½	tablespoon garlic powder	_____
☐	½	tablespoon ground ginger	_____

1. Cut racks into two or three rib sections. Season ribs with salt and pepper. Place oven rack in middle position. Preheat oven to 350°. Line a baking sheet with aluminum foil and spray foil with no-stick cooking spray. Place ribs in on baking sheet and cook in oven 15 minutes. Turn over, and cook another 15 minutes.

1. Combine remaining ingredients except ribs in a bowl and blend well. Taste, adjust flavoring.

2. Cut ribs into single rib pieces. Place ribs in slow cooker. Add sauce to slow cooker. Toss ribs to coat thoroughly.

3. Cover and cook 6 – 8 hours on low until done. Resist removing lid too often. Slow cooking requires internal heat and condensation. Internal temperature of ribs should be at least 160°.

NOTES:

Date: _____

RATE THIS RECIPE
○ ○ ○ ○ ○

NOTES

NOTES

APPENDIX

PLAYING WITH FIRE (INSIDE)

There are numerous methods for applying heat to food, thus turning it from tartar to terrific. Below are tips and tricks for effectively and safely performing this common-place yet profound metamorphosis indoors.

OVEN COOKING

Consider these tips:

- Oven mitts are mandatory and should always be kept where they are easily accessible. You run the risk of serious injury if you forget to glove your hand before thrusting said hand into the inferno of the oven and grabbing a hot handle.

- Preheating the oven is essential when following recommended cooking temperatures in recipes. If the oven is not at the recommended temp when you begin cooking the dish, the results may be less than palatable.

- Place the oven racks in the proper position before you preheat the oven. If you wait to move the rack after heating, you will be moving a hot oven rack and could potentially burn yourself.

- Double check the temperature settings before placing the dish in the oven.

- Utensils need to be ovenproof. If the tool is not ovenproof, it may melt when placed in a hot oven.

- When oven cooking with a sheet pan or broiling pan, line it with aluminum foil first. Spray the foil with no-stick cooking oil. Using foil will protect the pan from baked-on ingredients. Recipes with sugar products—white sugar, brown sugar, maple syrup, corn syrup or molasses—will burn hard onto the pan surface if it is not protected, sometimes to the point where it is easier to throw the pan out than clean it.

- Some recipes call for cooking the dish both covered and uncovered at different times in the cooking process. For best results, follow the instructions carefully.

Oven temperatures are often classified into categories. Here are the distinctions that I like to use:

250° – 300°	Low
301° – 350°	Medium
351° – 425°	Hot
426° – 475°	Very Hot
476° plus	Whatcha got yourself there, a nuclear reactor?

STOVE TOP COOKING

- The best stove top cooking happens when the correct size burner is used. Use small pots, pans and skillets on the small burners, and larger vessels on the larger burners.

- Make sure the temperature setting is correct. A high setting when the recipe calls for a low setting will ruin a dish quickly.

- Keep cooking utensils and ingredients in a location that won't require reaching across the burners or cooking vessels.

- When braising or sautéing food in a saucepan, the splattering of the butter or oil can cause serious burns. To minimize that chance, slightly lift the edge of the skillet that is closest to you and work with the ingredients at the back of the skillet.

- Consider when a lid cover or a splatter screen might be useful. Both minimize grease splatters, protecting you from burns. Bonus: will help keep the stove top and counters clean.

SLOW COOKER / CROCK-POT COOKING

The terms "slow cooker" and "crock-pot" are synonymous and refer to the same hardware. The lowest setting is generally about 200° and the high setting is about 300°. One cooking hour on high is roughly equivalent to two cooking hours on low. Many recipes that call for the "low" setting will go for approximately 8 hours, and if the recipes calls for "high," it is a good bet the recommended cooking time will be 3 – 4 hours.

To obtain the best dishes, the slow cooker must be no more than two-thirds full. Half full is fine. Steam creates a vacuum that seals the lid and the lid needs a tight fit to form a vacuum. If filled to the brim, the top will most likely not seal correctly.

Opening the lid prolongs the cooking time. Each time you remove the lid, it can add up to 15 minutes to the cooking time.

Some recipes suggest stirring the dish halfway through cooking. Stir quickly and replace the lid quickly.

Here are some tips for producing successful slow cooker dishes:

- Selecting cheaper cuts of meat is actually preferable when using a slow cooker. They have less fat, and the long, moist cooking turns what are normally tough cuts into tender treats.

- Remove poultry skin and excess fat. The fat melts with the slow cooking process and adds a distinctly unpleasant flavor and texture to the dish.

- Cut meat and poultry into cube pieces. This will ensure thorough cooking.

- Defrost foods before cooking.

- Foods at the bottom of the crock-pot cook at slightly higher temperatures. Pay attention to this when loading the vessel. For instance, when cooking a dish with meat and root vegetables, placing the vegetables on the bottom and the meat on top will help all the ingredients come to doneness at the same time.

- To ramp up the flavors, the liquid can be concentrated by cranking the slow cooker up to high for the last half hour.

- To prevent dairy products (sour cream, heavy cream, yogurt, milk) from breaking down, add during the last 15 minutes of cooking.

- The ceramic insert of the slow cooker can be damaged by sudden temperature changes. It should not be immersed in water while still hot from cooking, or taken from the refrigerator and placed into a preheated base.

- Exercise care when cleaning the ceramic insert. Let the insert cool before immersing it in water. Use a soft cloth and warm, soapy water to clean the insert. Do not use any harsh cleaners or abrasive cleansing pads. Do not immerse the slow cooker heating element or the cord in water, and keep the unit unplugged when not in use.

PLAYING WITH FIRE (OUTSIDE)

There is something primal about grilling food outdoors. The open air, the billowing fragrant smoke, the constant tending of the grill temperature, and the elaborate, almost ritual poking and prodding of the food. Below are tips and tricks for maximizing the grilling experience that have worked for me over the years.

ABOUT COALS

Open the vents on the bottom of the grill. Light a large chimney starter full of charcoal. If you don't own a chimney starter, I highly recommend you acquire one.

When the coals are glowing grayish white (start checking coals after 15 minutes), the coals are at their hottest. Spread the coals on the lower grate.

Positioning coals is critical for controlling the grill heat. Use long handled tongs to spread the coals around the lower grate. Leave a little space between coals.

THREE GRILLING METHODS

Here are three different tried-and-true grilling methods that are effective for just about any grilling situation. The methods are direct heat, indirect heat and tri-divided heat.

DIRECT HEAT

For even temperature distribution, spread the coals uniformly over the coal grate, at a depth of one or two coals. Open the bottom vents. Open the top vents if grilling with the cover on.

INDIRECT HEAT

This is the best method for barbecuing or slow roasting. The cooking is done with the grill covered and the meat grilled for an extended period, sometimes with wood chips to impart a smoked flavor.

Place an aluminum drip pan in the center of the charcoal grate. Light the coals and, when the coals are covered with gray ash, place the coals around the drip pan. Water can be added to the pan to provide moisture. Do not place meat directly over coals when grilling with indirect heat.

The temperature of the grill can be controlled by manipulating the upper and lower vents. The temperature for low-indirect cooking should be kept at approximately 275° for the entire cooking period. Use a grill thermometer to determine actual temperatures. If you are using wood chips, leave the cover slightly ajar to draw smoke upward over the meat.

TRI-DIVIDED HEAT

The third grilling method is to divide the coal grate into three sections. Place the coals that will provide the heat area for searing in section one, to the far left. The second section is a coal-free cooking area in the center, next to the burning coals. When grilling in the second section, the meat will not be directly above the coals. The third section of the grill is also coal-free and has less heat and is some distance from the coals. This is a good area for resting meats, and is an area to move the meat in the event of flare-ups.

GRILL HEAT CONTROL

Avoid lifting the grill cover too often. When the cover is lifted, the temperature drops significantly and the cooking time is extended. Use a grill thermometer to determine actual grill temperature.

HEAT TOO HIGH

If grill heat is too high, there are actions that can be taken to reduce the heat. The first is to use long handled tongs to scatter coals. Move the food to the coolest section of the grill. The vents, top and bottom, should be closed or nearly closed to starve the charcoal of oxygen.

HEAT TOO LOW

If the heat is too low, there are several things you can do to increase the heat. The first is to consolidate the coals by stacking them all in one place and adding more charcoal, preheated if possible. If the coals are not pre-heated, place the fresh coals on the hot collection of coals. Fan the coals with a newspaper. Lastly, open all the vents to provide plenty of oxygen.

If you are in a northern climate during the winter, clear the grill of any snow and provide more time for preheating. Increase the recommended cooking temperature by 15% – 20% to allow for the chill. Do not grill in an enclosed environment such as a basement or garage as deadly carbon monoxide gases can be trapped.

GAS GRILLS

Preheat all burners on high, cover the grill with the lid and heat for 10 minutes and then adjust heat according to recipe. For indirect heat cooking, turn off one burner. Turn off the middle burner if there are three. Always have a backup tank of gas.

GRILL SAFETY

- Place the grill well away from existing structures, deck railings, house eaves and trees.

- Place the grill a safe distance from other activities, especially foot traffic.

- Grills are designed to be used out-of-doors only. Indoor use poses both a fire hazard and the risk of carbon monoxide exposure.

- Always use long-handled grilling tools to give you plenty of clearance from heat and flames when cooking.

- Excess grease buildup in your grill is a fire hazard and will contribute to flare-ups while cooking, if not outright fire. Be sure to clean your grill periodically.

TRUE BBQ

Although the terms "grilling" and "barbecuing" are often used interchangeably, true barbecue is a process that can take from 12 hours up to several days, typically in the low, slow, gentle indirect heat of a smoker. Dry rubs, liquid injections and wood smoke flavor are often part of the equation. Though outside the scope of this cookbook, you may want to explore this wondrous process.

AVOIDING THE EMERGENCY ROOM

RUDE POISONING

Food poisoning (Food Borne Illness) is nasty and potentially deadly. Most preventable cases of food poisoning are caused by cross-contamination from raw meat, poultry, seafood and dairy products (a.k.a. "proteins").

Food safety issues occur when food is between the temperatures of 40° and 140° – the Food Danger Zone. Cooked food should never be allowed to remain in the danger zone for more than a couple of hours at most. Foods in the danger zone are a breeding ground for the bacteria and other toxins responsible for food-borne illnesses.

If food poisoning occurs in your home, take note of the foods eaten and then freeze any uneaten portions. The frozen samples may need to be tested in order to identify the offending bug and appropriate medical treatment.

When safety of the protein is in doubt, *discard it*. Always err on the side of safety.

SAFE HANDLING OF PROTEINS

- Refrigerate proteins promptly after purchase.
- Raw proteins should never be left out at room temperature.
- Packaged proteins can be refrigerated in the original packaging.
- Freeze uncooked proteins if they will not be used within 2 days.
- Proteins will take from 4 – 10 hours to thaw in the refrigerator. Do not thaw proteins on the counter top.
- To thaw proteins in cold water, place in a watertight plastic bag and change water frequently.
- The microwave can be used to thaw most proteins. Thawing seafood in the microwave is not recommended.
- Frozen, uncooked proteins such as meat and poultry should be used within two or three months of freezing. Frozen cooked protein should be used within a month of freezing. Freezing seafood – cooked or uncooked – is not recommended unless it is professionally frozen.

AVOIDING CROSS-CONTAMINATION

- Uncooked protein should be kept separate from produce, cooked foods and ready-to-eat foods.
- Never place cooked food on a plate that previously held uncooked protein.

- If you intend to use the marinade as a sauce, (1) keep a portion of the unused marinade separate for use on the cooked protein, or (2) place the used marinade in a sauce pan and bring it to a boil. Reduce heat and simmer for 4 – 5 minutes.

- Use one cutting board for fresh produce, such as vegetables and fruits, and a different one for raw proteins. If you must use only one cutting board, wash it thoroughly with hot, soapy water after using with raw proteins.

- Using hot soapy water, wash your hands, dishes, knives and other utensils thoroughly after coming in contact with uncooked proteins. For cutting boards and counters, use a hot soapy water scrub followed by a rinse solution of one tablespoon liquid bleach to one gallon water. Rinse with water.

COOKING TEMPERATURES

Cooking times listed in recipes are approximations. A meat thermometer is a necessary piece of cooking equipment for ensuring the proper internal temperature of foods. Always use this critical piece of cooking hardware to monitor internal temperatures.

See Table 5 in the Appendix[1] for recommended safe internal temperatures for cooked meats.

STOP, DROP AND ROLL

Cooking is the leading cause of home fires and home fire injuries in the United States. Taking proper precautions and learning what to do in case of a kitchen fire can prevent property damage, injury, and potentially save lives.

- Do not leave pots and pans unattended on the stove or in the oven. Most home fires are the result of unattended cooking. Turn pan handles on the stove towards the back to prevent food spills or children accidentally grabbing the handles.

- Pot holders and towels should be kept away from stove tops and ovens. Bathrobes, aprons and loose clothing are highly susceptible to catching fire. If clothing catches fire, immediately stop, drop to the ground and roll to smother the fire.

- In case of fire, turn off the burner under the burning pot or pan. Cover the fire with a large lid. Leave the lid on until the pan cools. Turn off the hood fan so fire is not drawn into the ducts.

- Always, *always* have a properly rated fire extinguisher within arms reach. Familiarize yourself with the instructions and practice a dry-run so you can operate it if and when needed.

- Never, *never* attempt to put out a grease fire with water. You will only cause the oil to erupt and this will spread the fire around the kitchen, and, in all probability, throughout the house. Use a Class B extinguisher.[2] (Most household fire extinguishers are Class ABC, so are appropriate.)

- Call 911 in the event of a fire.

NOTES

TABLES

TABLE 1: HERB AND SPICE SUBSTITUTIONS

RECIPE CALLS FOR	OPTION 1	OPTION 2
Allspice	cinnamon with a dash of nutmeg	dash of cloves
Basil	oregano	thyme
Cajun Spice	combine white pepper, garlic powder, onion powder, ground red pepper, paprika and black pepper	
Chili Powder	dashes of hot pepper sauce, oregano and cumin	
Chive	green onion	leek
Cilantro	parsley	
Italian Seasoning	blend of basil, oregano, rosemary and ground red pepper	
Cinnamon	nutmeg	allspice
Cloves	cinnamon	nutmeg
Cumin	chili powder	
Garlic, 1 clove	¼ teaspoon garlic powder	½ teaspoon prepared minced garlic
Ginger	allspice	cinnamon
Horseradish, 1 tablespoon fresh	2 tablespoons bottled	
Hot pepper sauce, 1 teaspoon	¾ teaspoon cayenne pepper plus 1 teaspoon vinegar	
Marjoram	basil	thyme
Mustard prepared, 1 tablespoon	1 teaspoon dry mustard	
Mustard dry, 1 teaspoon	1 tablespoon prepared mustard	

RECIPE CALLS FOR	OPTION 1	OPTION 2
Mustard Dijon, 1 tablespoon	1 tablespoon dry mustard mixed with 1 teaspoon white wine vinegar, 1 tablespoon mayonnaise, and a pinch of sugar	
Nutmeg	cinnamon	ginger
Oregano	thyme	basil
Parsley, ¼ cup chopped fresh	1 tablespoon dried parsley flakes	¼ cup chopped cilantro
Poultry Seasoning	sage plus a blend of thyme, marjoram, black pepper, and rosemary	
Red Pepper	dash of hot pepper sauce	black pepper
Rosemary	thyme	tarragon
Sage	poultry seasoning	marjoram
Thyme	basil	oregano

TABLE 2: COMMON INGREDIENT SUBSTITUTIONS

RECIPE CALLS FOR	ALTERNATIVE
Broth, beef or chicken, 1 cup	1 bouillon cube dissolved in 1 cup boiling water
Coconut milk, 1 cup	3 tablespoons canned cream of coconut plus enough milk to equal 1 cup
Cornstarch, 1 tablespoon	2 tablespoon all-purpose flour
Corn syrup	honey
Cream, half-and-half, 1 cup	½ cup whole milk, plus ½ cup light cream
Cream cheese	cottage cheese, puréed
Green onions	onion
Honey, 1 cup	1¼ cups sugar plus ¼ cup liquid
Leeks	shallots
Lemon juice	vinegar
Maple syrup, 2 cups	honey, 1 cup
Mayonnaise, 1 cup	½ cup yogurt and ½ cup mayonnaise
Mushrooms, 1 pound fresh	6 ounces canned mushrooms
Oil (sauteing), ¼ cup	¼ cup melted butter
Onion, 1 medium	1 tablespoon dried minced onion
Red Pepper	dash of hot pepper sauce
Sour cream, 1 cup	1 cup sour milk and ¼ cup butter
Sugar brown, 1 cup firmly packed	1 cup granulated sugar plus ¼ cup unsulphured molasses
Tomatoes, 1 cup canned	1½ cups chopped tomato, simmered for 10 minutes
Tomato juice, 1 cup	½ cup tomato sauce plus ½ cup water
Tomato ketchup	1 cup tomato sauce plus ½ cup sugar and 2 tablespoons vinegar
Tomato sauce, 2 cups	¾ cup tomato paste plus 1 cup water
Vinegar, Balsamic	sherry vinegar
Vinegar (white or cider)	lemon juice
Worcestershire sauce	bottled steak sauce

TABLE 3: HEALTHY INGREDIENT SUBSTITUTIONS

RECIPE CALLS FOR	HEALTHY ALTERNATIVE
Bacon	turkey bacon, ham, Canadian bacon
Butter	60/40 butter blend with reduced calorie margarine
Cream	skim milk, evaporated skim milk
Cream cheese	yogurt cheese
Egg, 1 whole	2 egg whites
Egg, 2 whole	1 whole egg plus 2 egg whites
Ground beef	ground poultry
Heavy cream, 1 cup	1 tablespoon flour whisked into 1 cup nonfat milk
Mayonnaise	half light mayonnaise and half non-fat yogurt
Meat	legumes, lentils, dried beans or dried peas
Milk, whole	2% milk, 1% milk, skim milk, evaporated milk or soy milk fortified with calcium
Sour cream, 1 cup	1 cup low fat cottage cheese plus 2 tablespoons skim milk plus 1 tablespoon lemon juice
Tuna, canned, oil-packed	canned tuna, water-packed
White bread	100% whole grain or 100% whole wheat bread

TABLE 4: LIQUOR SUBSTITUTIONS

RECIPE CALLS FOR	OPTION 1	OPTION 2
Amaretto	almond extract	marzipan
Apple brandy	apple juice	apple cider
Apricot brandy	apricot preserves	
Beer or Ale	chicken broth	ginger ale
Bourbon	sparkling grape juice	vanilla extract
Brandy	raspberry extract	brandy extract
Champagne	ginger ale	soda water
Cognac	peach juice	apricot juice
Coffee liqueur	espresso	coffee syrup
Creme de Menthe	grapefruit juice	mint extract
Grand Marnier	orange marmalade	orange juice
Peppermint Schnapps	mint extract	mint leaves
Port	cranberry juice plus lemon juice	
Rum	pineapple juice	vanilla extract
Sherry	apple cider	coffee syrup
Vermouth	apple cider	
Vodka	white grape juice plus lime juice	apple cider
Wine, Red	grape juice	cranberry juice
Wine, White	white grape juice	apple juice

TABLE 5: SAFE INTERNAL TEMPERATURES

CUT	MINIMUM SAFE INTERNAL TEMPERATURE
Roasts – Beef, veal, lamb	145° F (medium rare) 160° F (medium)
Fish, shellfish	145° F
Pork	160° F
Ground – beef, lamb, veal	160° F
Egg dishes	160° F
Poultry, any cut	165° F
Leftovers, any meat	165° F

TABLE 6: TRINITY FLAVOR BASES

TRINITY	1	2	3
French (Mirepoix)	celery	onion	carrots
Cajun or Creole (Holy Trinity - 1:2:3 ratio)	onion	bell pepper	celery
Italian	tomato	garlic	basil
Mexican	ancho chili pepper	pasilla chili pepper	guajillo chili pepper
Chinese	scallions	ginger	garlic
Greek	lemon juice	olive oil	oregano
Indian	garlic	ginger	onion
Spanish	garlic	onion	tomato
Thai	galangal	kaffir lime	lemon grass

TABLE 7: PEPPERHEAD SCALE

PEPPER	SCOVILLE HEAT UNITS
Cherry	500
Sonora	600
Coronado	1,000
Polano	2,000
Ancho	2,000
Anaheim	2,500
Chipotle	5,000
Jalapeño	10,000
Serrano	22,000
Tabasco	50,000
Cayenne	50,000
Jamaican Hot	200,000
Chocolate Habanero	425,000
Police Pepper Spray	5,300,000
Pure Capsaicin	16,000,000

TABLE 8: RECOMMENDED RIB GEAR

GEAR	DESCRIPTION
Aluminum foil	12-inch wide works well for lining the baking pan and for covering the ribs after cooking.
Baking pan	A rectangular baking pan is used for baking ribs and sauces together. A heavy duty pan that will not warp works best.
Basting brush	A heavy 2-inch silicone brush with a comfortable 8-inch handle works well.
Extra bag of charcoal	Never run out, never say die
Extra LP tank	Never run out, never say die
Fire Extinguisher	One in the kitchen, one by the grill
Grill thermometer	Helpful for regulating grill temperature.
Heavy knife or heavy scissors	Used for cutting the rib segments. The heavier and sharper the knife the better. A rigid knife works well. An industrial-strength pair of scissors sometimes works better than a knife for segmenting ribs.
Measuring cup	A measuring cup registering standard increments.
Measuring spoons	A complete set of measuring spoons from 1/8 teaspoon to a full tablespoon.
Meat thermometer	Essential for determining when the ribs are ready to safely eat.
Mixing bowls	Various sizes used for mixing sauces and marinades.
Oven mitts	Used for protection when extracting items from the oven and when working the grill.
Re-sealable plastic bags	Used for coating and marinating ribs.
Rib rack grill accessory	Holds multiple rib racks in vertical position.
Saucepans	Used for preparing sauce. Saucepans with heavy bottoms work best.
Short- and long-handled Tongs	Used for extracting ribs from marinade and for turning ribs when baking and grilling.

GEAR	DESCRIPTION
Skillets	Used for braising and sauce reduction – a large skillet for braising and a smaller one for sauces. I recommend a stainless steel skillet with an aluminum core.
Spatula	For stirring and coating ribs. Spatulas with tips rigid and large enough to mix and coat a lot of ribs at a time work best.

REFERENCES

[1] Excerpt from USDA Keep Food Safe! Food Safety Basics
http://www.fsis.usda.gov/factsheets/Keep_Food_Safe_Food_Safety_Basics/index.asp

[2] U.S. Fire Administration, Fire Extinguishers
http://www.usfa.dhs.gov/citizens/home_fire_prev/extinguishers.shtm

NOTES

INDEX

S

Sauces. *See* barbecue sauce; *See* black
        bean sauce; *See* brown sauce;
        See chili sauce; *See* duck sauce;
        See fish sauce; *See* hoisin sauce;
        See oyster sauce; *See* plum sauce;
        See steak sauce; *See* tomato sauce
sauerkraut 120
scallions 32, 62
seasoned salt 82
sesame oil 62, 104, 118
sesame seeds 83, 118
shallots 113
sherry vinegar 58
soy sauce 32, 42, 44, 53, 59, 62, 67,
        89, 91, 96, 98, 99, 101, 104, 113,
        115, 118, 130
steak sauce 36, 44, 66
sweet sherry 98

T

thyme 44, 58, 61, 64
tomato paste 105, 106, 108
tomato sauce 61, 68
turmeric 113

V

vanilla extract 72
vinegar 50

W

whiskey 56, 72, 74, 106, 108
white sugar 80, 94, 104
white vinegar 44, 105
white wine 44
Worcestershire sauce 31, 36, 44, 52,
        56, 59, 64, 66, 74, 92, 96, 101,
        106, 108, 115, 116, 126, 128

NOTES